Apostles of Silence

Apostles of Silence

THE MODERN FRENCH MIMES

Mira Felner

RUTHERFORD ● MADISON ● TEANECK
FAIRLEIGH DICKINSON UNIVERSITY PRESS
LONDON AND TORONTO: ASSOCIATED UNIVERSITY PRESSES

Associated University Presses
440 Forsgate Drive
Cranbury, NJ 08512

Associated University Presses
16 Barter Street
London WC1A 2AH, England

Associated University Presses
P.O. Box 338, Port Credit
Mississauga, Ontario
Canada L5G 4L8

Library of Congress Cataloging in Publication Data

Felner, Mira, 1947–
  Apostles of silence.

  Bibliography: p.
  Includes index.
  1. Mimes—France. 2. Mime. I. Title.
PN1948.F7F44 1984   792.3'092'2   83-48682
ISBN 0-8386-3196-7

Printed in the United States of America

For Richard

CONTENTS

PREFACE

Defining a visual genre like mime in a literary medium is an awesome task, more difficult than discussing other plastic arts that leave tangible evidence of their form. Since no text exists for these performances, their form can only be inferred from the impressions of critics: to my regret, reviewers provided little descriptive material. However meager its substance, every attempt was made to include as much physical description as possible.

The majority of the sources consulted were French newspaper reviews (originating in Paris unless otherwise noted). These were obtained from the scrapbooks at the Bibliothèque de l'Arsenal in Paris. The primitive system of cataloging there created certain problems in documentation. Articles were clipped from newspapers and magazines in a haphazard manner that often resulted in the cutting off of the author, title, publication, or date in various combinations. This explains the absence of such material in footnotes and bibliography. From time to time, there was an attempt made by the librarian to rectify the omission by writing the pertinent information in fountain pen on the absorbent scrapbook or newsprint paper. These entries, most likely barely decipherable from the start, have become more illegible with the smudges of time. Where possible, I made educated guesses at the original content, an easier game with well-known publication titles than with the names of the obscure critics who wrote for them; at that, the proliferation of newspapers in postwar Paris made even the title guesses a chore. When the inked-in data appeared more like a Rorschach test than bibliographic material, I opted for omission. Dates were the most trustworthy of all the information given, for the scrapbooks were arranged in chronological order, and it is easy enough to document performance dates through programs and biographic data. Despite the obstacles, I made every attempt to keep inaccuracies to a minimum.

All translations are by this writer unless otherwise noted. Where published translations existed, I compared them to the original source for accuracy. In cases where such translations failed to capture the nuance of the original, I provided my own translation. Punctuation is as close to the original French and Italian as possible.

Since the four mimes studied in this book are men, as were most of the major figures in the history of this art, I have chosen to leave general references to these performers in the masculine gender. I believe this makes for stylistic clarity and consistency, and in no way indicates my lack of appreciation for the many talented women mimes who continue to contribute to this art form.

It was my studies with Jacques Lecoq that inspired this work. I would like to thank M. Lecoq for the fabulous creative experience through which he expanded my vision of the theater. I am most appreciative for the interviews he accorded me, and for the use of his personal notes and private library.

To the late Jean Dorcy, Etienne Decroux's movement teacher at the Vieux Colombier, I owe special recognition. Beyond the fount of information on the origin of mime in the work at the Vieux Colombier that he gave me during formal interviews, M. Dorcy, almost eighty years old, demonstrated exercises from strenuous gymnastics to refined mime techniques. His vibrance, his energy still reflected their source in his work with Jacques Copeau over fifty years ago. Jean Dorcy represents to me the incarnation of the creative spirit and zeal of the Vieux Colombier. Over a glass of wine in a Paris bistro, he shared with me personal anecdotes and tales of the intrigues of the men who are studied here, adding a dimension of human interest to this work. One evening, we went together to see Marcel Marceau at the Théâtre de la Ville. Dorcy, the teacher of Decroux, sat beside me as we watched Decroux's most celebrated protégé. That night, the past and present were one.

ACKNOWLEDGMENTS

I would like to thank the following for permission to publish photographs: The Cultural Services of the French Embassy, Lee Lamont of ICM Artists, Ltd., Jim Moore, Stanley Allan Sherman, and Etienne-Bertrand Weill.

I am grateful to Professor Michael Kirby for helping me to maintain my objectivity in this endeavor. I wish to acknowledge the invaluable assistance I received from Tony Brown, Louise Jensen, Tom Leabhart, and Kari Margolis, as well as a special debt to Professors Edwin Wilson of Hunter College and Laurence Wylie of Harvard University for their support and encouragement. Thanks are due Susan Suslak and Sally Small for their careful preparation of this manuscript, despite the challenge of disorganized copy and constant changes and additions, and George Lynch for his cogent editorial assistance. To the librarians of the Performing Arts Research Center at Lincoln Center of the New York Public Library goes my appreciation for their patient service during the preparation of this book.

The deepest gratitude I owe to my husband Richard for his critical insight, marathon babysitting, and most of all, for his sustaining love.

11

Apostles of Silence

1

INTRODUCTION

The ancient mime tradition had so dissipated by the turn of the century, that it appeared an exhausted art. The last fifty years have witnessed a worldwide resurgence of the form. The apostles of silence—Etienne Decroux, Jean-Louis Barrault, Marcel Marceau, and Jacques Lecoq—are responsible for this renaissance of mime in the twentieth century. These four Frenchmen are descendants of a long and venerable tradition, yet each believes he has created a new approach to the art and seeks to distinguish his work from the mime of other eras. This work analyzes their individual contributions toward defining a new mime aesthetic.

Mime: An Art in Search of a Definition

It is difficult to define *mime,* for what is denoted by the term is different for each generation. As a form, it is as old as man and has evolved with him. It is a genre whose source of expression lies in the mutable physical being, leaving little tangible evidence of its form and content. More than any other idiom, its style is the product of the mime himself, changing with each actor and subject to the definitions of the individual performer. The root of the definitional problem lies here. If mime is the product of the individual, then, given the transitory nature of man and the evanescence of his corporeal being, mime defies the lexicographers' attempts to fix its ever-changing form.

15

The definitions of mime in the *Oxford English Dictionary*[1] that directly parallel those found in the French *Robert,* in no way elucidate what the mime form is, and in many ways even compound and obscure the problem with inaccuracy and ambiguity. They tell us only that mime is an all-encompassing term, referring to the player, the play, the form, the historical style, and the action. This in itself is significant, for it indicates the vital link between the performer and the medium in mime.

The relationship between the form and the performer is the key to understanding the cyclical nature of mime. With the death of the great mime of each era, the form has died as well. It lives in the shadows of other arts, waiting for some new genius and resuscitation. Each rebirth yields a mutant form. Until this century, the techniques of mime have been intransmissible, defying codification. Much of this phenomenon can be attributed to a deliberate attempt by the mimes to keep the techniques a trade secret. As with other trades, whatever skills were communicated from generation to generation were kept within the family, passing only from father to son as a carefully guarded heirloom.

If the nature of mime is so transitory that it eludes simple definition, then another approach must be used in analyzing this genre. Through speculation on a series of questions, some generalizations about the form will be attempted.

Is mime an art? The spontaneous response is yes. Mime is considered an art form today, but if we trace its historical roots, the question is not so simply answered.

Anthropologists Alison Jolly and Marcel Jousse believe that mime in its mimic form was born with the dawn of human life, when in the absence of language, man first gesticulated to communicate. If such gesture was mime, then, it was not art, and is not mime now, for to this generation the term implies a conscious artfulness and creative process. Mutes may mime, but they are not mimes: so the verb is different from the noun.

The first record of mime as an art form occurs in ancient Greece. It is known that there were troupes of mimes with organized performances as far back as the sixth century B.C., yet Aristotle, writing *The Poetics* in the fourth century B.C. gives no attention to that genre, saying only that "Comedy was not seriously pursued at first . . . it was performed by volunteers, and its various forms had developed before the time of those

who are called comic writers and are remembered. . . . Comic
plots originated in Sicily (Epicharmus and Phormis). . . ."[2]

Allardyce Nicoll states, "The most famous name associated
with the early mime is that of Epicharmus,"[3] and that he "invented comedy in Syracuse at the same time as Phormus"[4]; the
two originators of comedy to which Aristotle refers were therefore mimes and writers of mimes. Although mime was performed during the era of Aristotle, after citing it as the source
of comedy, he does not deal with it ever again. Does this imply
that Aristotle did not consider mime an art form worthy of his
analysis? One can only speculate on this point, but the evidence
indicates that he did not take it seriously. Aristotle believed that
both comedy and tragedy had moral and didactic value. But as
Nicoll points out, mime had an "unmoral (or secular) attitude,"[5]
and this may have rendered it unworthy of his theorizing.
Thus, early in its history, a clear distinction is drawn between
comedy and mime. Plato takes an even more conservative view
of the moral nature of art, claiming that one should "set himself
against performers who give the audience pleasure in wrong
and improper ways."[6] But it is precisely from Plato that we
learn of the great pleasure the Greek public took from these
performances.

Mime was therefore a popular entertainment in antiquity
and continued as such through the nineteenth century. It was
performed in many different contexts: as intermezzi and exodium pieces, in circus arenas, in connection with medicine
shows, road shows, on the streets, and in palaces and private
homes, where mimes hired themselves out as court fools. Mime
was clearly spectacle in each of these cases, but was mime art?
Did the people who patronized it consider mime to be an art
form? This is an impossible question to answer, for the masses
do not write critical works to be analyzed centuries hence, and
popular entertainments were not the primary province of aesthetic theorists of past generations. We only know that mime
was spurned by philosophers and the church, but adored by the
general public.

This raises a complex aesthetic issue often debated today: Is
the vernacular culture art? With the growing emphasis on current popular culture, the trend leads to a simple categorization
of ancient mime as art. But this does not reveal how it was
regarded in its time. Although our era has elevated most popu-

lar forms of entertainment, ironically, modern mime, in general, falls more and more in the domain of the esoteric. Theorists take an elitist view of its contemporary manifestations demanding a fixed aesthetics and formal technique. In fact, Jean Dorcy, the only person to attempt an overview of the subject in the twentieth century, refuses to call the acrobatic Greek and Roman style, reborn in the Commedia, "mime."[7] He believes modern mime to be a higher art.

It remains that mime is considered a conscious art form today; thus, for the purposes of this book, it will be considered as such, leaving the question of its categorization in times past as one open to speculative judgments. If mime is an art, then it is clearly a performing art, but beyond that, how can its form be delineated?

Today it is considered solely as a corporal art, but it is known that this was not always so. There has, however, always been great emphasis on the body in this genre. In the nineteenth and twentieth centuries it was labeled a mute art, but much controversy exists over the necessity of silence. An examination of mimes past and present reveals that mime was and is not always silent. The Greeks, the Romans, the Commedia, all used language in their performances. It is significant that words are always a secondary source of expression when integrated with mime, and that gesture always holds the more prominent role. This is in direct opposition to traditional drama. It can therefore be said, that although language was often used, mime is more a corporeal than a literary art, and as such is often an improvisational form, not being bound to a fixed text of primary importance to the spectacle.

Even for those to whom mime is a silent art, it may not necessarily be an art in silence; for music and sound effects have often been an integral part of the mime performance.

Defining mime as a corporal art does not clarify its form; for to move the body is not mime. There are other corporal arts with which it can be confounded. It is therefore essential to differentiate among mime, acrobatics, and dance.

Dance as art is born early in the anthropological acculturation process. Its origin lies in ritual and as an explanation for mystical phenomena. It is the pure expression of internal states, of the organic unity between man and nature. It has been documented that the danced Dionysian rites led to a dance theater in ancient Greece, where slowly the word took precedence over *movement*.[8] As the culture developed, the dance form evolved into mime and theater. Although there were ancient mimic dances that narrated explanatory tales of mystic events, mime as an art form is a more conscious act than primitive dance, occurring at a different time in the acculturation process; mime tends to be more social than religious or spiritual—it is a less direct form of expression.

Despite this attempt to clarify the difference in the origin of mime and dance, anthropologist Marcel Mauss claims the area of distinction between mimic and sentimental dance to be insufficiently drawn and the point at which dance becomes so narrative as to become mime to be unclear.[9] It can be said only that the primitive dancer tends to be animated by a spirit, moved by some superior force; whereas the mime has always been motivated by worldly impulses, even in his earliest performance.

The Greek and Roman mimes were clearly commentators on society. They often revealed the basest aspects of humanity, and were rooted in the mundane world. Mime dealt with social man, dance with his spirit and soul. This was the traditional emphasis until the twentieth century. The new mime believes it can do both.

This examination of origins needs to be supplemented by some generalizations about form. Until this century, mime attempted to tell a story that was generally comic. Although classical dance shares this narrative quality, it is less often comic, and the historical view of dance reveals that it has just as frequently been performed for its pure expressive nature. Dance has always been an evocative form; but mime is most often realistic, and less often symbolic. Whereas dance is rhythmic, mime may be rhythmic, nonrhythmic, or intentionally antirhythmic. Whereas dance is concerned with aesthetics, mime may be aesthetic, nonaesthetic, or intentionally antiaesthetic when it serves its message to do so.

Although mime and dance have evolved, mime movement has defied codification until the twentieth century; whereas dance has had canons and conventions of set movements for hundreds of years. Dance requires this formalization, for it is primarily a group activity, and the ensemble performance requires a common technical language. Also, a dancer's prowess is measured by his or her ability to interpret a proposed aesthetic. But mime, as stated, is a solo art, subject to more individual criteria and personal inspiration. Even in the sparse records of ancient mime, names of individual performers are hailed, isolated from any troupe recognition. In modern times mime has moved towards codified movement and evocative gesture, and dance has moved towards mime's earthliness and away from a totally fixed aesthetic.

Although both mime and acrobatics require physical prowess, in acrobatics the feat requiring muscular coordination and strength is an end in itself. When acrobatics is integrated with mime performances, it becomes a vehicle for emotional expression and is no longer the mere demonstration of virtuosity typified by the circus or gymnastic events. In mime, all movement should reflect the inner life of man. Jacques Lecoq explains:

> Pantalon, in a rage, would make a dangerous reverse somersault, without performing a demonstration of an acrobatic exercise. The somersault was not visible in and of itself, but it was part of the architecture of anger, and the audience only felt the overwhelming rage of Pantalon.[10]

Acrobatics is a tool of mime, but it loses its identity when used as such, becoming only a vehicle for expression of character, and not a demonstration of physical virtuosity.

Despite this attempt to distinguish among mime, dance, and acrobatics, they are so often integrated with each other that the divisions between them remain unclear. Although there is an overlapping of form and an ensuing problem in determining differences, they vary clearly enough in origin and function so that it is intuitively felt that in referring to mime, one does not mean a branch of dance or gymnastics. There is an inherent sense of the independence of mime from these genres. Still, the autonomy of mime has not been established, for many still believe it to be an integral part of dance or theater.

It has been established that mime is a performing art, a corporeal art different from dance and acrobatics; but can it be concluded that mime is independent of the theater as well? Until recent times the question went unasked, now it seems to be the source of great controversy. It has in fact been an issue creating dissension in the ranks. The four mimes who are the subject of this work disagree as to the answer.

Mime has traditionally been considered a popular entertainment, but are all popular entertainments theater? Is the circus? Mime has been performed inside and outside the physical theater itself, so approaching the problem from the scenic perspective offers no solution. It has from time to time been integrated into the performances of plays: does that make it theater? Analogously, dance is often performed in an opera; does that dance lose its identity as dance and become opera? Most often mime is performed independently; but does that make it autonomous? Mime is performed by mimes and not by actors. An actor is not necessarily a mime, but is a mime an actor?

These questions are provocative, but provide no concrete answer to the problem. The issue has been debated for years, and this work will content itself with an exposition of the answers each of the great mimes discussed here established for himself as a basis for his individual aesthetic.

One thing is certain: the modern renaissance of mime began when Etienne Decroux proclaimed mime an autonomous art, independent of dance, theater, or any other form, and set out to establish an independent body of theory and technique. A new era of mime was launched.

It appears that the more one attempts to define mime, the more it seems to elude definition. Its ephemeral quality prevails. It is in this light that the examination of the contemporary French renaissance of mime must be made, seeking not for sweeping definitions of the art, but an understanding of the individual renditions of the form. Each great figure in today's world of mime has redefined the idiom according to his needs and talents. They have all found personal answers to the questions posed in this chapter. This work will provide an exposition of their individual solutions.

The extent to which Decroux, Barrault, Marceau, and Lecoq are truly proponents of a new art can be verified only through analyzing their work in the perspective of history. To this end, it is in order that a brief retrospective of the art of mime be provided. It is not the goal of this work to furnish a detailed history of the subject. It is rather to provide a basis for stylistic and technical comparison of the twentieth-century mime phenomenon and an orientation point for the reader. This history will attempt to trace the evolution of the mime form.

Mime: A Retrospective

It is assumed by anthropologists that primitive man engaged in some kind of gesture language for communication purposes, and that this language became a supplementary one when an oral tradition developed. In some cultures, ritual gave way to dance, often to mimic dance, then to mimic legend.[11] These are the two earliest forms of mime. But at this point in the acculturation process, mime is not considered a professional occupation, nor as an art form, but merely a part of some necessary communication process.[12]

The first evidence of mime as an independent and conscious art form occurs in Megara. Aristotle cites the time as 581 B.C., but scholars believe this form to date from at least two hundred years earlier. It is also known that a similar form developed in Sicily in the fifth century B.C.

These early mime shows were gay, improvised amusements. The actors wore tights and padded custumes, were often masked and phallephoric. Nicoll believes the use of the phallus and ensuing lewd tone suggest that these performances were linked to Dionysian revelry. Unlike the serious comedy and tragedy of the time, the mimes were nondidactic in purpose, and in fact, usually burlesqued divine legend. It was clearly a secular genre.

The Greek mime was a total theater. There were song and improvised texts that often parodied comedy and tragedy. The spectacle consisted of a panoply of physical entertainments: juggling, acrobatics, magic, dance, and mimic gesture. There were mini-dramas of the comic pranks of stock characters. In many ways Greek mime resembles the combination of forms found in the music hall performance.

There is some evidence of written texts, but where these were used, they were only the basis for improvised gesture around the scenario. Despite the use of dialogue, it appears that the emphasis in these shows was on broad physical humor, and that gesture was the primary vehicle for expression.

The ancient mime troupes were usually itinerant, which explains the geographic spread of the form. The performances varied from theatrical events, to street shows, to private entertainments, or interludes and exodium pieces during dramatic representations.

Dorian settlers brought the form to the Italian mainland and

provided a bridge between Megara and Rome. These improvised plays and players were called *Phylakes* for the Roman town
of their origin. Later the Atellan farce from the Oscan City of
Atella, formalized the stock characters of Greek and Roman
mime in short written sketches.

In the later days of the Roman Empire, the form became so
popular as to rival traditional theater and even usurp the role
of classical comedy. There is some evidence of a composite
form developing, consisting of textual narration of comedies
while *joculatores* mimed the action. This mime action was literal
and denotative gesture.

Concurrent with the Roman mime, a new genre developed—
pantomime ("all-miming"). This was a form of interpretive
dance. Indeed, its performers were called *saltatores* ("dancers").
Music and song were used as in mime, but the major difference
appears to be the totally silent nature of the pantomime. All the
actors wore masks representative of particular characters.
These were different from those worn by the mimes in that
they had no mouth openings. The closed mask is the strongest
evidence of the silent nature of pantomime. The mood of pantomime was more somber than that of mime. Although they
often dealt with the same subjects, the pantomime was serious
in its treatment, the mime, lighthearted and merry. It is assumed that this accounts for the greater popularity of mime
over its less-spirited competitor.

There are two anecdotes that give some insight into the form
of the ancient pantomime. The first tells of an actor named
Livius Andronicus (third century B.C.), who having lost his
voice, refused not to perform. He had his slave recite the text of
the performance, while he mimed the action that corresponded
to the words.[13] Silent mime—pantomime, was thus born
through defect and default. The second tale

According to a certain Roman writer, a foreign monarch
once witnessed at the court of Nero a pantomime in which a
famous actor enacted all twelve labors of Hercules with such
clarity and expression that the foreigner understood everything without a word of explanation. He was so amazed by
this that he asked Nero to make a present to him of the actor.
Nero was extremely surprised at such a request, but the guest
explained that on the border of his kingdom there lived a
savage people whose language nobody could understand and
who, in their turn, could not understand what their neigh-

bors wanted of them. By means of mime this famous actor could convey the king's demands to the savages without any risk of misunderstanding.[14]

Both anecdotes affirm the narrative nature of pantomime and its literal interpretation of reality.

Thus in ancient Rome, mime and pantomime were two distinct genres of popular entertainment. It will be interesting to trace the evolution of both forms and their eventual crisscrossing of styles, resulting in the interchangeability of terminology in the nineteenth century.

As the mimes had ridiculed the gods of Greece and Rome, so in turn the Catholic church became the victim of their wit. For this reason, most medieval documentation of the tradition occurs in the form of clerical criticism of the players and their shows. This does affirm, however, that some forms of popular entertainment persisted through the Middle Ages. There is evidence of a secular drama reminiscent of the Atellan farce, and it is speculated that the jongleurs and troubadours did more than just juggle and sing, but were in fact direct descendants of the itinerant classic mimes, who continued presenting mini-mime dramas with stock characters similar to those represented in earlier forms. It is speculated that the masked mummings grew out of the mime tradition, and that there were elements of pantomime in the mystery plays as well.

There are various opinions as to the exact fate of mime during the Middle Ages. The only certainty is that, in contrast to its widespread popularity for centuries, the mime form was relegated to a minor role in medieval culture. More than a thousand years went by before it was resuscitated. During the fourteenth and fifteenth centuries, the Atellan farce was reborn, and out of this genre evolved the Commedia dell'Arte.

Although there is no concrete evidence that the Commedia is a direct descendant of the Greco-Roman tradition, there are so many marked similarities between the two forms, in masks, costumes, and stock types, that it seems inconceivable that there be no link between them. This has led many mime historians to the belief that the mime was somehow kept alive during the Dark Ages, and that the open spirit of the Renaissance allowed it to blossom once again. It is possible, however, that the similarities are accidental, and that universal character types are born anew in each era.

The improvisational nature of the Commedia dell'Arte is inherent in its very name, for *arte* refers to the special art of improvisation that could only be performed by skilled professionals who could act without text. This was juxtaposed against the Commedia sustenuto traditional drama that could be acted by amateurs because it depended on a fixed text. The Commedia was treated as any other craft: there were masters, apprentices, and families transmitting the skill from generation to generation. Actors often played the same role their entire lives.

The subjects of improvised sketches were arranged before performances. Once on stage, the actors improvised around the given theme. There were, however, certain standard *lazzi*— comic stage business, to which the actor would turn for comic effect. These ranged from pure slapstick humor to acrobatic stunts, all guaranteed to get a laugh. The existing records of the lazzi indicate that they placed great physical demands on the performer:

> In the Italian Comedy, the body possessed not just great expressive value, but there was also a great deal of importance placed on strength, agility, and physical suppleness, which the actor demonstrated in pure acrobatic numbers which went beyond expressive intentions. . . . The Commedia dell'Arte conserved this acrobatic element throughout its evolution.[15]

The Commedia was also the only Renaissance theater that preserved the tradition of the mask. "The mask naturally served to intensify the expressive power of the body. . . . For when the spectator sees a masked actor on the stage, he fixes his attention on the body, and grasps with much more intensity the force of the body's mime."[16] Many clear parallels between the Commedia and the classical mime are apparent: Both were improvised, masked, required great physical skill, integrated music and song, and used a text only as the basis for broad physical humor.

The Commedia themes and characters grew out of Renaissance humanism. Each mask signified a stock type representing a particular foible. The scenarios demonstrated the complexities of human needs: hunger and love were the primary subjects of Commedia performances.

The Commedia troupes traveled the continent. They were

the favorites of kings and common people alike, playing palaces and street corners. Their popularity was so great that they came to exert an influence on the written drama as well. Commedia plots and characters appear in many of the plays of the late Renaissance. For the purposes of this book, it is the effect of the Commedia in France that is of greatest consequence.

The Commedia dell'Arte provided a brutal counterpoint to the French précieux drama of the seventeenth century. The Commedia troupes swept over France, easily rivaling domestic theater for popular acclaim. This immediate success is a great testimony to the physical prowess of the Italian players, for

> when the first Italian companies came to France they played in their native tongue, but they had of necessity inherited the traditions of their art to such a degree that they were able to make their Parisian audiences understand them without difficulty by virtue of their clever mimicry.[17]

This contemporary account of a Commedia performance in France confirms the pantomimic skills of the Italian actors:

> The incomparable Scaramouche . . . served as a model for the difficult and necessary art of simulating all the passions and expressing them solely through the play of the features. It was in this pantomime of terror, indeed, that he made his audience rock with laughter for a good quarter of an hour, without once opening his mouth to speak. He possessed this marvelous talent to such a remarkable degree that it is easy to understand how he could, by the mere promptings of his remarkable imagination, wring the heart strings more effectively than any orator could ever hope to do, even with all the resources of a most persuasive rhetoric at his command. . . . A prince who once saw him play in Rome was so moved by the force of Scaramouche's art that he exclaimed admiringly, "Scaramuccia non parla, e dice gran'cose!"[18]

The Scaramouche described here is Tiberio Fiorillo, who spent much of his life in France and greatly influenced French theater. "Molière, who had the highest opinion of Fiorillo, lost no occasion of seeing him on the stage and took him as the model for his interpretation of Sganarelle. . . ."[19] This led Molière to incorporate more of the Commedia techniques into his plays.

The description of Scaramouche's performance indicates that the Commedia in France was often totally mute and sometimes as serious in tone as the Roman pantomime. It is usually assumed, however, that the spirit of the Commedia was closer to the classic mime tradition. This description raises the possibility of a synthesis of form between mime and pantomime in the sixteenth century, for both the French pantomime and mime can clearly trace their origins back to the Commedia.

Gradually the Italian scenarios were replaced by French scripts. The Italians learned French, and French actors joined the Commedia troupes. The Commedia became less and less improvisational as it blended with the French literary tradition. By 1760, there were almost no Italian-born Commedia players in France.[20]

While the Commedia dell'Arte was the rage of Europe, England remained relatively unaffected by the Italian players. In 1573 and 1574, Italian companies were denied licenses to perform for the Italian Catholic actors were unwelcome in Anglican England. The Ravenna troupe, granted permission to play some ten years later, failed to appeal to the British sense of humor. There is some evidence that Commedia-style entertainment appeared at fairs in the seventeenth century. However, in 1673, after the Restoration, when Tiberio Fiorillo arrived in London, he was an enormous success. His imitators multiplied and Commedia characters began to appear in British dramas.

By the eighteenth century, an English pantomime form was developing. John Weaver (1675–1760) had begun work on a silent ballet pantomime. This was really more a narrative dancing of stories with mythological themes. Weaver's work was to contribute to the form of nineteenth-century ballet. It was actually John Rich (1692–1761) who created the lasting English pantomime form that was a combination of Weaver's ballet pantomime with the Commedia dell'Arte. This strange marriage of styles thrived for over one hundred years.

The basic outline of the new pantomime with its emphasis on spectacle, rarely varied.[21] It opened with the dramatization of a myth or fairy tale until some magic figure, such as a fairy godmother appeared and waved a magic wand, miraculously transforming all the characters into the stock types of the Commedia dell'Arte. Some standard Commedia scenario would proceed— usually Harlequin in love with Colombine, opposed in this affair by Pantaloon and his servant. All sorts of violent encounters would occur in a series of tableaux, until Harlequin would whirl some magic weapon and defeat his enemies. All this could not occur without a knockabout chase scene that thrilled the audience and was the most vital part of the Harlequinade. The chase served as a pretext for acrobatic stunts: use of stilts, pratfalls, tumbling, contortions, and leaps. In the midst of the dialogue, dance and song were interspersed. Eventually, there was some magic resolution of both plots: love was requited, peace and harmony restored. Magically, the Commedia characters were metamorphosed back into the mythological figures of the first story. The English pantomime form was therefore able to flit from subject to subject, getting a laugh where it could with no regard for the laws of logic or the principles of Aristotle.[22]

The growth and popularity of the English pantomime form was fostered by political events and licensing laws. The British government rigorously controlled the number of legitimate theatres permitted to perform spoken dramas. To fill the need for more entertainment, new theatrical genres developed that circumvented these restrictions. In England in the mid-eighteenth century, theaters could obtain a Burletta license that permitted musical dramas in three acts, use of rhyme, song, dance, and comic numbers accompanied by the orchestra. The Licensing Act of 1737, which restricted the performance of plays not licensed by the Lord Chamberlain, did not apply to pantomime. These regulations encouraged the development of the pantomime form.

The great figure of English pantomime was Joseph Grimaldi (1778–1837) whose character "clown" usurped Harlequin's position as the dominant character.[23] The clown character had appeared on the British stage before, but only as a rural clod, a country lout, the lowest creature of this type. Until Grimaldi, clown was used as a generic term, and clowns had no traditional role or stage business. Grimaldi transformed the generally unsympathetic "clown" into "Clown,"[24] a new stock character of English pantomime. The country bumpkin became the cosmopolitan wit. Still a servant, he was impudent, irreverent, and unrepentant. He mocked and played dirty tricks on his betters. The new working class of urban London could identify with this persona who became the hero of the deprived as they cheered him on in his mischievous pranks. His public affectionately called him "Clown Joey."

Grimaldi spoke and sang. In fact, Clown was the most vocal of all the characters in the pantomime. Grimaldi's songs were known by all and often contained vulgar innuendo.

Grimaldi gave Clown stock traits—gluttony, lust, and theft—tarts and sausages were his favorite targets. Grimaldi fashioned distinctive makeup and costume for Clown. To the traditional whiteface he added two bright red triangles on the cheeks, heavily colored lips and eyebrows, a comic wig, ornamented shirt, garters, and baggy pants with big hidden pockets for stolen goods. The physical attributes of Grimaldi's clown have served as the basis for clown costumes since his invention. The influence of Grimaldi's comic vision is unmistakable. Grimaldi grew into a biting satirist of current follies. Under Grimaldi, the Harlequinade became the most important part of the pantomime sequence.

Grimaldi performed in large theaters where a broad acting style developed of necessity: slapstick, rough-and-tumble knockabout humor was the order of the day. The daring physical stunts were designed to please at a distance. Makeup and costumes helped the effect. Theater size altered most dramatically the need for scenic effects. The pantomimes were staged as extravaganzas where fantastic stage illusions, magic transformations, elaborately constructed sets, and devices for gags and stunts were the rule.

After the death of Grimaldi and an unsuccessful attempt by his son to continue the family tradition, British pantomime declined in popularity. No heir apparent to his Clown Joey appeared. So dependent was the Harlequinade on Grimaldi's talents that the form itself faded into obscurity. Its demise was hastened by the liberal Theatre Regulation Bill of 1843, which eliminated restrictions on performance. Within years of Grimaldi's death, the music hall and other variety shows supplanted pantomime in popularity.

The eighteenth century witnessed government repression of the theater in France as well. After the revolution, Napoleon ordered the closing of all but the four state theaters and four recognized Boulevard theaters. The latter were only permitted to perform short comedies, melodramas, and pantomimes. As new theaters were allowed to open, each was given a carefully prescribed style of performance, usually precluding the use of dialogue. The theater remained a place for the elite, and the general public turned to street fairs for entertainment. The fair was a variety show: medicine men (thériacleurs), circus, magicians, and Commedia-style sketches all combined to create a festival of popular entertainment.

In 1815, with the reestablishment of the monarchy, strict censorship continued. Pantomime troupes petitioned the government for permission to use even one spoken line on stage.[25] Under these conditions, it was inevitable that a pantomime form would flourish.

A new style developed that met the mandatory order of silence, incorporated dance, and as such was similar to the Roman pantomime; but its use of stock characters, lazzi, acrobatics, and general spirit of merriment resembled much more the Greek and Roman mime and the Commedia. At this point the terms *mime* and *pantomime* come to be used interchangeably, and, indeed, the form created out of political necessity is a composite of the two.

The nineteenth-century French pantomime style, known as *la pantomime blanche* (for the white facial makeup of the zany) is a result of the artistry of Jean-Gaspard Deburau, who set the standards for all pantomime performers.[26] Deburau was born in Bohemia in 1796 and came to France in 1811 as part of his family's aerial and acrobatic circus act. Hired by the Théâtre des Funambules—one of those Boulevard theaters housing curious variety show entertainment—Deburau played the part of the clumsy clown to set off the graceful feats of the rest of his family. The theater management grudgingly accepted Deburau as part of the family contract. In 1818 he was a reticent last-minute replacement for the actor playing the Pierrot character in one of the pantomimes. Apparently, he was such a hit that evening that a legendary career was launched.

In France, as in England, Harlequin had been the central character in all the pantomimes. Deburau, like Grimaldi, shifted the relative importance of this character. Deburau's Pierrot became the focal point of all the action. But his was not the Pierrot of the past—a mentally deficient, naive, clumsy, rustic recipient of kicks.

Pierrot first appeared as a French character in 1665 in Molière's *Don Juan*. Molière claimed to have consciously copied the Paillasse of the Italian comedy, making the necessary changes to develop him into the stereotypical French peasant.[27] Until the nineteenth century and Deburau, he remained nothing more than

a poor zany . . . the ever available target for mockery and scorn, and suffered not only from the contemptuous kicks and insults heaped on him by the grander members of his family, but was forced to submit to much baiting from the audience whose play in this was almost a convention.[28]

Deburau metamorphosed the status of the Commedia character, making Pierrot into a hero of the lower class, as his comic pranks claimed aristocratic victims. He adapted old Commedia scenarios to his own needs, diminishing the roles of the other characters, improvising relevant social and political satire.

> Deburau's Pierrot was always a victor, never a Pierrot. Jean-Gaspard aggrandised, enlarged and betrayed his role. It finished by being the entire play, and this is said with all the respect which is owed to the memory of the most perfect actor ever to exist. But Deburau alienated Pierrot from his origin and denatured him. Under the flour and helmet of the illustrious Bohemian, Pierrot took on the air of the master and an aplomb that did not fit. He now gave the kicks and received no more.[29]

This contemporary account of the Deburau Pierrot underscores just how much Deburau broke with the zany of the Commedia. His was the Pierrot of another era: "He became king of the Boulevard du Temple; the king who had once been a slave. His popular triumph expressed emancipation related to the glory of the new democrat."[30]

Deburau modified Pierrot according to his own personality. The gluttony, theft, violent sexuality, and general debauchery of the past were refined into gourmet overeating, theft for justice à la Robin Hood, and gallant seduction. His practical jokes bore an air of satiric jest. The distribution of violent blows appeared to be his right. Pierrot became an aristocratic clown. The passive boob Pierrot became the active champion of the new republican. Deburau became the hero of his public as Grimaldi had been to his London audience.

Deburau adapted the traditional Pierrot costume. Tall and reedlike, his body could easily be exploited for comic effect. He covered his slender frame in a billowing chemise and baggy pants. He exposed his overlong neck by removing the traditional ruffled collar. Portraits all emphasize the comic value of his giraffelike quality. He covered his head with a tight-fitting black cap that dramatically set off his whiteface makeup. The result—a theatrically striking costume, both comic and poetic in feel, permitting ease of movement. Deburau, like Grimaldi, often played Pierrot in the guise of other stock characters. At these times, he too changed his habitual costume to some comically conceived spoof of contemporary social types.

The French pantomime form was a more unified genre than its British counterpart. It usually had one single line of action and was unencumbered by subplots. The plot went through innumerable complications in a series of tableaux. The central character's woes multiplied into a seemingly insurmountable situation. Through wit, cunning, and pranks, he achieved a reversal of fortune in the climactic scene. All ended well in a pat denouement. This form enabled Deburau to fully display his talents for stunts, acrobatics, and physical effects.

Although this aggressive Pierrot broke with the stereotype, Deburau's style did not. It remained one of broad physical humor, always comic, continuing the use of the standard gags of the Commedia lazzi. Deburau, however, was always silent. Title cards were therefore displayed to help the audience situate the dramatic action. The mask removed, Deburau could resort to mugging to express actions and emotions without words. This kind of exterior expression indicates that Pierrot remained a superficial, nonpsychological, external character. Tristan Rémy, Deburau's biographer, confirms that

> this Pierrot, as with all mimes of the Commedia dell'Arte, does not interpret different characters. Whatever occurs, these mimes play their own image, their own unique role. . . . Deburau, condemned to mutism by the police laws, expressed what a popular audience without a rich vocabulary could understand.[31]

The Deburau pantomimes were not totally improvised, as was the Commedia. George Sand wrote, "This seemingly spontaneous fantasy was prepared with extraordinary care."[32] It is known, however, that Deburau did improvise some physical gags and dance numbers. Deburau's humor was the playing of contradictions. Often, he maintained a precarious balance between consummate grace and awkward clumsiness. He would bow gallantly to a maiden, then behind her back indicate some sexual liberty he would like to take with her. As a gentleman clown, he'd knock you down and then take you to the hospital. Eyewitnesses claim he mixed a quality of poetic fantasy with robust comedy. This mixture of buffoonery and elegance was the magic of Deburau.

To the end of his days, Deburau was the darling of the Parisian public. His performances lured the intelligentsia and the aristocracy to the Funambules, formerly the terrain of the lower classes. Given the rigid social barriers of nineteenth-century Paris, it is a credit to the art of Deburau that the elite would even deign to frequent a theater previously designated for the lowest social echelons.

Deburau remained silent long after the repeal of the laws banning dialogue. He knew where his virtuosity lay and was not about to compromise it. In a letter to George Sand (who had written to Deburau to inquire about his failing health), he wrote, "My pen is like my voice on stage, but my heart is like my face."[33]

After the Napoleonic wars, various British performers came to Paris. Among them were brothers Clément-Philippe and John Laurent who brought *la pantomime anglaise* to the stage of the Funambules. The English form was used for several pantomimes, and eventually a rivalry developed between Deburau and the elder Laurent, who played Harlequin. In the end, Deburau kept his position as the central character, but worked within the English pantomime style and story line. More acrobatic and knockabout humor was used. The most important English innovations were elaborate technical stunts, visual stage effects, transformation scenes, and spectacle. Laurent is credited with introducing this style at the Funambules.[34] *Comédie d'accessoire* replaced comedy of situation and sentiment.

As was customary, upon Deburau's death in 1846, his son Charles inherited his father's Pierrot character and continued to work in total silence, even after repeal of the laws banning speech. Eyewitness Maurice Sand recounts: "The Pierrot of Charles was the most beautiful and elegant Pierrot ever to exist."[35] But Charles was less exuberant in style and depended less on acrobatic lazzi. Of the Pierrot of Paul Legrand who studied with Deburau père, Sand writes: "He was less physically gifted but handsome and full of ideas and comic inventions and was particularly distinguished by an ability to produce pathetic and dramatic effects."[36] Another observer of Legrand states:

This was no longer the surprising, daring Pierrot of Deburau but a good child, with tears in his eyes, ready to laugh. We had never seen Pierrot cry on the stage, but Paul's success was immense the night we saw two real tears roll down his snow-white mask.[37]

These accounts indicate the gradual dissipation of the *pantomime blanche* and its hero Pierrot into romantic sentimental-ism. The physical exuberances and comic pranks inherited from the Commedia disappeared. Rémy believes that while De-burau dealt with basic human needs expressed through a stereotype, Legrand expressed sentiments, and that there is a debt owed to Legrand for having put pantomime into the liter-ary dramatic tradition, creating the genre of melo-pantomime.[38] This appears to be a misguided judgment that ignores the vitality of the ancient tradition of stereotypes and lazzi. On the other hand, Paul Hugounet, writing in 1889, says, "Pantomime, brought to such heights by Deburau, will descend to the depths with him."[39] This seems to be a case of the art perishing with the artist. Severin, the last mime Pierrot, con-tinued the sentimental tragic rendition of the Paillasse. The vibrant zany was transformed into the melodramatic Pierrot noir. The tombstone was placed on the French *pantomime blanche* when, in 1883, Sarah Bernhardt played Pierrot.

The pantomime tradition continued on a minor scale in the provinces, but it never attained the mass appeal it had known from the Renaissance through the lifetime of Deburau. Many of the old pantomimists returned to the spoken word and found outlets for their talents in the circus-clown and as music-hall comedians.

The early days of this century were the time of a totally dissipated mime-pantomime tradition. The broad stylized com-edy was replaced in France on the Boulevard by melodrama and bourgeois naturalist plays, in England by the music hall, and in Italy by the circus. The people's entertainment as a theatrical form for twenty-five hundred years seemed to have perished. Charles Dullin summed it up well:

It was an art too tied to the complexion of the individual actor not to be subject to the fate of all living bodies: Birth with a primal scream into a state of semi-consciousness, an impetuous adolescence, irresistible in its spirit and momen-tum, a maturity conscious of the power obtained through the acquisition of wisdom, then old age . . . the old age of the dying clown.[40]

The silent film was born, and technological limitations caused a revival of pantomimic art. Once again, of necessity, mime-pantomime became a popular genre. The music hall performer—Charlie Chaplin—and the circus entertainer—Buster Keaton—returned to the mime form. Dullin talks of the close family relationship between Charlie Chaplin and the Italian comedy.[41] Chaplin, the symbol of the craft, revived the Deburau tradition, creating a socially relevant, triumphant comic character. Others returned to the Commedia zany type of eternal victim. The mask was gone,[42] but the acrobatic humor, the plot as pretext for physical comedy, the narrative gesture returned. Still the comic hero remained physically invulnerable. Although his situations were realistic and representational, he, unlike his real-life counterpart, was capable of surviving everything nature or technological society can set against him: train wrecks, explosions, cave-ins, waterfalls—he always emerged untouched. The film mime maintained the archetypical character of ancient mime.

Although the cinema continued to call back the old mimes from the circus and the music hall, the live stage seemed to ignore the ancient form. The ancient art languished, awaiting new life.

2

JACQUES COPEAU
(1879–1949)
The Origins of the New Mime

The early twentieth century was a period of sclerosis in the actor's art in France. The star system engendered ham acting, distortion of text, and lack of ensemble playing; naturalism was often used as a pretext for poor technique, amateurism, and lack of poetry and style; and the Comédie Française promoted an archaic denatured vision of the classics. After years of written protests against this state of affairs, a young drama critic, Jacques Copeau, believed he could resuscitate the theater. If the art were being destroyed by a cult of personality and commercial interests, then Copeau felt, its revitalization lay in a new theater based on craft and humanism. In September of 1913, he published a manifesto—"An Essay of Dramatic Renovation: the Théâtre du Vieux-Colombier"[1]—a statement of purpose and principles that would guide him and the group of enthusiastic young actors he had assembled. They shared his vision of a purified theater, stripped of the trappings of commercialism, and dedicated to the work of a creative ensemble. The company of the Vieux-Colombier began a search for, and originated, new stage techniques that inspired French theater and mime for decades to come.

It is not the purpose of this chapter to chronicle the legendary accomplishments of Jacques Copeau, but rather, to examine those aspects of his work that contributed to the modern mime

36

form. We are concerned here with the years between 1914 and 1919, when Copeau's ideas were crystallizing, and from 1920 to 1929, when his school functioned as a laboratory for the innovative movement training that served as the inspiration for the proponents of the new mime. Copeau's ideas were germinating during a period of ideological turbulence, as theater artists responded to the general sense of stagnation of forms. Copeau fell under the influence of several men whose revolutionary concepts helped guide his path.

His visit to Gordon Craig's school in Florence, during the fall of 1915, shaped a new awareness of the potential of the physical stage.[2] Craig convinced him that the new stagecraft necessitated new materials and forms that could be discovered only in a school that functioned as a creative laboratory. Believing in the necessity of technical perfection, Craig espoused the idea of several years of apprenticeship without public performance; however, Copeau disagreed, sensing that a public airing was a vital part of the experimental process. The two men concurred that the key to revitalizing the theater lay in developing a sense of craft among theater artists. Their meeting pushed Copeau further toward the development of a school. He wrote:

> It is neither talent nor ideas that are lacking, nor heart, nor need. It is the discipline of craft which once reigned over even the most humble endeavor. It is the rule that to think well leads to the ability to do well, competency with perfection in mind. Art and craft are not two separate entities.[3]

Craig, of course, believed the designer and director were the keys to the renewal of the theater, even wishing to rid the stage of actors altogether, believing their technique too uncertain. He proposed replacing them with giant marionettes.[4] Copeau shared Craig's dismay at the faltering craft of current actors, but nonetheless believed them to be the most essential element of theater. Therefore, the hope of the future lay in the perfecting of acting technique. They were both fascinated by the potential of the use of masks.

Craig's symbolist concepts revealed to Copeau that theater could express poetic and symbolic values only if the minimum and essential objects were put on stage. This meshed perfectly with Copeau's idea of the "treteau nu," the bare stage, where the drama and poetry created by the mere presence of the actor in space could be emphasized. Copeau believed this "nakedness" provided the proper background for displaying acting technique.

Copeau traveled from Florence to Geneva to meet with Emil-Jaques Dalcroze, who provided him with his first insights into the role of corporal training for actors.[5] Dalcroze had created eurhythmics—a method fusing gymnastics and pantomime with music in order to release a child's natural instinct for rhythm, movement, and play. After observing Dalcroze's students act out *Snow White* while Dalcroze read the text to a rhythmic piano accompaniment, Copeau wrote:

> This link with music, this musical aid, I see it within the education of the actor: the interiorization of music in the organs, in all the active faculties to obtain precision and freedom.[6]

At first, Copeau believed eurhythmics was the key to movement for the actor, but he eventually became disenchanted with the method, noting that text preceded movement and led to unnatural gesture. Copeau believe the actor should proceed from immobility and silence to movement, then sound, words, and text, in that order. Eventually, his training program systematized this progression.

Dalcroze introduced Copeau to the Swiss designer, Adolphe Appia who had been working on new scenic concepts.[7] Appia believed musical time should determine action, movement, and design, providing an integrated and harmonious production concept. From him, Copeau culled the idea of a unified art work, but Copeau conceived that a mise-en-scène should not be united by music, but through the spoken word, through the rhythms of text and emotion that are comparable to those of music and can dictate the form of a production. As music suggests sounds, and sound suggests the word, Copeau believed emotion could be achieved through intonation.[8]

Appia perceived the three-dimensional quality of the stage. He taught Copeau that "the plasticity of the human body on the stage, developed by rhythmic training, and shown to advantage by the malleability of the set design can be highlighted by the judicious use of light."[9] Appia conceived of the stage in relation to dramatic action. His view that the actor may be lit like a piece of sculpture opened new insights for Copeau into the role of corporal expression.

Appia, like Craig, was interested in renewing the theater through design. Copeau's last documented words to Appia were:

> What shocks me, and worries me, is that you and Craig, you are building the theatre of the future without knowing who will live there, what kind of artist you will put on the stage, or house in the very theatre you wish to welcome them. It seems to me, Appia, that I alone have begun at the beginning in taking on the job of forming a troupe of actors.[10]

From Constantin Stanislavski, Copeau learned of the importance of sincerity and truth, that action must be linked to a psychological state, that movement should originate from need. Copeau called him "the master of us all"[11] and modeled the Ecole du Vieux-Colombier on Stanislavski's studio. When Stanislavski arrived in Paris in 1922, he and the members of the Moscow Art Theatre visited the Théâtre du Vieux-Colombier, leading Copeau to say, "His very presence consecrated our work-place."[12]

These four men helped shape Copeau's ideas and direction during his formative period. From each of them he took what was essential to his purpose, but the product of his work bears his personal stamp.

During World War I, Copeau was sent to the United States by the French government as a cultural ambassador. His lecture tour brought an invitation to bring his troupe to New York. Copeau spent a difficult two years in New York, working under less than ideal creative conditions, shaping his repertory to American commercial interests. He did, however, use this time to continue his research in actor training. Actress Suzanne Bing, who was to become Copeau's master teacher, worked in a Montessori nursery where she closely observed children at play for a better understanding of instinctive and natural movement.[13] This experience served as an inspiration for acting exercises that she later developed. Upon his return to Paris, Copeau reopened his theater and, in February 1920, began his theater school.

The goal of the Ecole du Vieux-Colombier was to form a "poet of stagecraft." If the theater was to reflect a new humanism, then the actor must be formed as a total human being— nurtured intellectually and spiritually, and given the power to physically express his emotions. To this end, Copeau created a program that provided "the technical training, the complete education which was apt to develop harmoniously the student's body, spirit and character."[14] The curriculum of his school demonstrated this balance, offering courses in theatrical theory and criticism, civilization, theater history, and design; traditional conservatory courses in acting, diction, language, poetry and prosody, voice, and music; and an incredible gamut of classes in corporal expression: acrobatics, mask, mime, and choral work, improvisation, circus skills, dance, and Hébertisme. The number of courses in movement training reflects Copeau's view that

> The method should follow the natural development of the instinct for play in the child, encouraging this, giving him focal points, procuring for him the means for self-expression according to his taste, imagination and need for entertainment. First we must give him an obedient body. Then one draws out of gymnastics the concept of interior rhythm, then to music, dance and masked mime—to the word, to elemental dramatic forms, to conscious play, to scenic invention, to poetry.[15]

This was the first time so much emphasis had been given to physical training in a French acting school. The decision to do so not only reflects Copeau's understanding of the body as the actor's primary tool, but is representative of new concepts gaining increasing acceptance. The French system of physical education had been revolutionized by a new series of books by Georges Hébert—*L'Education Physique du l'entrainement complet par la méthode naturelle,* which underscored the general physiological atrophy afflicting modern man.[16] It was exactly this atrophy as it manifested itself in the theater that had moved Copeau to start his school.

Hébert presented a scathing sociological examination of contemporary man's alienation from his body. He claimed that our muscle tone and reflexes have been so deformed by society and fashion that total physical reeducation is necessary in order to regain natural movement. Espousing a noble savage theory (echoing Rousseau), Hébert believed that man in his natural state followed normal muscular development, learning to use his body efficiently to cope successfully with nature's environment. As society grows more complex, man's interaction with natural stimuli is limited, and the now-obsolete physiological mechanisms atrophy. In order to counterbalance the effects of modern technology on the body, Hébert developed a system of exercises that provided for consistent and total corporal development. Implicit in the acceptance of Hébert's ideas is the acceptance of a new aesthetics, based on an unstylized view of physical beauty, independent of all sense of fashion.

For Copeau, Hébert's system facilitated the goal of "the natural development of the instinct for play," through the building of physical prowess and the regaining of instinctive behavior—two vital tools for the Copeau actor.

Hébert himself was a member of the faculty at the Vieux-Colombier until he was replaced by one of his trainees. Eventually, Jean Dorcy taught the exercises in Hébertisme in conjunction with classes in circus skills. He told of going to the Medrano Circus each day to work with and watch the Fratellini Brothers, famous clown acrobats of the era. He would then return to the Vieux-Colombier to teach the day's new techniques.[17]

The work in acrobatics, circus skills, and Hébertisme broadened the actors' range of movement, improving coordination and flexibility, and thereby serving as a cornerstone for more elaborate techniques.

The more advanced movement classes focused on the development of kinesthetic awareness, maskwork, improvisation, and stylized movement. The most basic of these was the course in kinesthetic development taught by Mme. Bing that dealt with "notions of space and movement, . . . force and duration, place, orientation, balance, lightness, heaviness, gentleness, elasticity, resistance, direction, . . . obedience and independence, . . . the musical sense."[18] Exercises were designed to make the student aware of "the feelings accompanying an action."[19] To develop an inner sense of rhythm and phrasing, children's songs were sung and mimed with changes in rhythmic patterns and dynamics. The students would build to a crescendo and find the appropriate changes in movement to accompany the changes in voice and rhythm. Rhythm was used as a link among the actors as a means of uniting choral movement, and also served as a bridge to text.

In another set of exercises, students were asked to mime wind, rain, trees, clouds, and other natural phenomena.[20] This freed the performer, expanded his range of physical expression, stimulated the imagination, and provided a strong sense of environment that could be brought to scene work. The work progressed from abstract elements to imitation of animals where the student sought to discover "shape, movement, rhythm and sound" through "observation and imitation."[21] The animal work evolved into the enactment of La Fontaine's fables. Here physical animals were expanded into animal characters.[22] This was a stepping-stone to more complex characterization.

The actors worked towards subtle emotional articulation through movement. They were asked to respond to questions with either willingness or restraint demonstrated only through gesture.[23] There were isolation exercises where only one part of the body was used to express changes in emotional state and given circumstances. Integrating his work, students played charades that evolved into the miming of myths, that became final production objects and were linked to their academic work in Greek studies.[24]

Suzanne Bing developed a series of exercises that resemble what we call theater games today; these were inspired by her work in the Montessori school in New York.[25] They were designed to free the "child-like instincts for play," break down blocks, and release spontaneous movement. Copeau developed an exercise that tied this work together:

> He threw us a word: "Paris," "storm," "The Goal" etc., etc., and we had to react immediately without a moment of reflection with one of several gestures, by a pose, by a sequence of movements, etc.[26]

This segment of the training reflects the emphasis Copeau placed on improvisation as a necessary acting technique. In fact, when directing, he spent lengthy rehearsal periods giving the actors freedom to improvise around the text. From their spontaneous creations he culled the central concept for his mise-en-scènes.

Perhaps the most innovative segment of the movement training was the work devoted to masks.[27] Copeau believed that all the great ancient styles of theater used masks. To understand the essence of theater, he believed it necessary to look back to the origins of Western drama in the masked choral work of Greek tragedy, which he called "the mother cell of all dramatic poetry."[28] To Copeau, the mask represented the quintessence of theatrical transformation and provided the key to the actor's approach to the role. He was the first person in this century to recognize its psychological force:

> The virtue of the mask is even more convincing. It symbolizes perfectly the position of the interpreter in relation to the character, and demonstrates how the two are fused one to the other. The actor who plays under the mask receives from this object of cardboard the reality of the character. He is commanded by it and obeys it irresistibly. Barely has he shoed the mask, when he feels pouring out of himself a being of which he was unaware, that he did not even suspect existed. It is not only his face which is altered, but his being, the character of his reflexes where feelings are being formed which he would have been incapable of imagining with his face uncovered . . . even the accent of his voice will be dictated by the mask—by a persona—that is to say by a *personnage* without life as long as it is unwedded to the actor, which came from without, yet seizes him and substitutes for the self.[29]

Further, as Jean Dorcy underscores,

> With the face hidden, we have only the body with which to express our thoughts and make them understood, and we are therefore forced to evaluate the importance of this tool.[30]

Waldo Frank, the noted author, critic, and chief American correspondent for *La Nouvelle Revue Française,* after a visit to Copeau's school in Burgundy, made this observation on the virtue of mask work:

> He puts a mask upon the pupil's face. He permits him to use his voice not in speaking or in singing, but in a sort of primitive gamut of onamatopoetic sounds. The body must express the idea, masked and muted. The voice of the beginning is a kind of arabesque like the castanet in the classic Spanish dance. But even before the body may express the simplest emotion or idea, it must learn to express *forms.* The pupils of Copeau are taught to articulate what might be called the Platonic essence of a tree, an animal, an ocean. This must come ere they be deemed worthy aspirants for the creating of a man. Similarly, their voices must learn to do without words, in the establishing of pictures or of passion, or even of complex human situations. The props of story, set, verisimilitude of facial gesture and of spoken word are taken from them: so

that in their graduation to the high plane of literary drama they may be energetically freed to establish in the *word* the distinctions and elaborations which are the essence of true poetics.[31]

Before beginning mask work, the student was expected to obtain a state of inner peace, of openness that readied him to take on the character of the mask. The state of immobility and silence are key to Copeau's technique:

> The departure point of expressivity: The state of rest, of calm, of relaxation, of silence, or of simplicity . . . this affects spoken interpretation as well as playing or action . . . to start from silence and calm. This is the first point. An actor must know how to be silent, to listen, to respond, to stay still, to begin an action, to develop it, and to return to silence and immobility.[32]

This state of immobility was seen as a preparation time for the action that was to follow. It facilitates neutralizing the self and opens the actor to new emotions. Copeau acknowledges that there are different tones of immobility and calm that reflect what is to follow. Even in calm and stillness, there is never emptiness. This is the lesson he wished his actors to learn.

Mask exercises were progressive. The first step was to begin a proper readying process. Jean Dorcy described the "rites" he followed before "shoeing" the mask:

> Here are the rites I followed so as to be ready to perform masked:
> a) Well seated in the middle of the chair, not leaning against the back of the seat. Legs spaced to ensure perfect balance. Feet flat on the ground.
> b) Stretch the right arm horizontally forward, shoulder high; it holds the mask, hanging by its elastic. The left hand, also stretched out, helps to shoe the mask, thumb holding the chin, index and second finger seizing the opening of the mouth.
> c) Simultaneously, inhale, close the eyes and shoe the mask.
> In all this, only the arms and hands are active. They carry out the small movements necessary to fasten the mask on the face, arrange the hair, verify the proper adjustment of the

elastic, so that the mask will cling well and hold without slackness.

d) Simultaneously, breathe and place forearms and hands on the thighs. The arms, as well as the elbows, touch the torso, fingers not quite reaching the knees.

e) Open the eyes, inhale, then simultaneously close the eyes, exhale and bend the head forward. While bending the head, the back becomes sightly rounded. In this phase, arms, hands, torso, and head are completely relaxed.

f) It is here, in this position, that the clearing of the mind occurs. Repeat mentally or utter, if this helps, during the necessary time (2, 5, 10, 25 seconds): "I am not thinking of anything, I am not thinking of anything. . . ."

If, through nervousness, or because the heart was beating too strongly, the "I am not thinking of anything" was ineffective, concentrate on the blackish, grey, steel, saffron, blue, or other shade found inside the eye, and extend it indefinitely in thought: almost always, this shade blots out conscious thought.

g) Simultaneously, inhale and sit upright, then exhale and open your eyes.

Now the masked actor, sufficiently recollected, can be inhabited by characters, objects, thoughts; he is ready to perform dramatically.

This was my method. One of us (Yvonne Galli) achieved this clearing of the mind, this preliminary state, better and more rapidly. Had she another Sesame? I have never asked for her technique.

When the actor is not seated but standing, nothing changes; however see e), the back should not be rounded, for the weight of the head would draw the torso forward.

All these phases are for beginners. Later, the technique may be altered. But this recollection is so important that, in my opinion, it should never be neglected.[33]

At first, students make their own masks from a variety of materials. This produced a wide gamut of expressive masks. Copeau felt it was important to create a neutral mask that would take its expression from the body of the actor, thus placing more emphasis on corporal expression. At this time, sculptor Albert Marque was brought in to help design such a mask.[34]

The first silent mask exercises were simple explorations of emotional states: "Tiredness, hunger, sunworship, fear," among others.[35] The students discovered that masked movement broke down emotional barriers. Their simple actions were mimed as well as natural elements. Later, more complex masks were used: fantastic nonhuman masks were the bridge to expressive masks. This work eventually led back to characterization.[36]

Waldo Frank describes the results of the work he witnessed at Copeau's school:

The scene is bare, let us say, save for a table. A boy jumps on this, masked. He is portraying a tree in a sunny field. He is not acting a pantomime: he is improvising a drama; and the first factors to convince are his associates. His arms and body, marvelously swaying, convey the shady scope of bole and branch moving in a breeze. A wayfarer enters (like all the others, masked). He espies the shade and goes to it, escaping the heat of the sun. He sleeps. Enter a flock of sheep. (These are boys and girls on all fours, costumeless, of course). They see the tree, nibble at its leaves, seek its shade. They come in collision with the man. Man and beasts are frightened off. . . .

A group of pupils come to the front of the stage. They must produce, despite their masked faces, a vision of a strand and of fisherfolk peering out upon a stormy sea. Their bodies create not alone their own emotion, but by a subtle fugue the heave of the water. A rowboat comes up. It is created by two actors in a rhythmic unison of propulsion. They leave their boat and mount the stairs to the apron. They have news of the drowning of a comrade: the news transfigures the group. The scene shifts to what is an interior of a fisher cottage. The wife and children await the master. The friends come in, with the tragic tidings. . . .

The stage is a crowded street in Paris. A naughty poster rouses the risibilities of the *bonnes femmes*. A gendarme interferes and tries to tear down the poster: he has to cope with the vigorous protests of the *bons becs de Paris*. (No word is spoken, no face is seen, there is of course no "business" on the bare stage, nor has there been a preamble of explanation.)

Now, these little acts, primitive as they are in Copeau's work, go already beyond pantomime and diverge radically from the dance. They have, indeed, a rhythmn and ideal movement, as have the dance and music. Rhythm is precisely the undifferentiate, common element of art. But these scenes are a beginning of drama. The so positive silence, the so poignant dimensional lack which are the traits of pantomime give way here to an essential, socially dimensioned fullness.

Copeau seems to be proving what may one day appear a
fundamental law in the revised theatre which we all expect;
that the essence of drama is symphonic: that it exists unitarily
in a single form of which body, body movement, body group
and voice plasticity are ingredients; and of which the Word is
a sort of constant zenith possessing the ideal, serene quality
of a culmination.[37]

Frank believed Copeau's work surpased the literal narrative
pantomime form of the nineteenth century. The work he describes is imagistic and capable of connotative meaning.

The theatrical style that permitted the synthesis of all these
techiques was the Commedia dell'Arte. In this form, mask work
and improvisation unite with essential voice and movement to
create a total art. Although his initial interest was awakened by
Craig, Copeau claimed to have been led back to the Commedia
through the plays of Molière, where the characters, lazzi,
rhythm, and style of the Commedia had been preserved.[38]
Copeau studied in depth the classic art that he believed to be
the soul of European theater. He believed the renewal of the
theater could be sparked by a renaissance of the humanism of
the Commedia in a modern context. He proposed

to invent a dozen modern characters, archetypes of great
scope representing personalities, faults, passions, social and
moral fools (ridicules), people of today. To invent their costumes and silhouettes which would remain forever the same
modified only by circumstances or props.

These ten characters of an autonomous comedy which
could encompass all genres from pantomime to drama would
be given to ten actors. Each actor would have a character
which would become his property, who would become one
with himself whom he would nourish from within through
his own feelings, observations, experiences, readings, and inventions. Here is the great discovery (so simple)! The great
revolution, or rather, the great and majestic return of the
oldest tradition. A brotherhood of farceurs always playing
and improvising together—authors, actors, singers, musi-
cians, and acrobats (only clowns today are a survival of this
form). These ten characters would put themselves through
all possible changes. There would be infinite meeting points,
constant renewal, it would be the rebirth of satire and gaiety.
There you are! It is no more difficult than that—No sets,
always the same props and immutable physiognomy. I al-

ready see three of these characters: the Intellectual (doctor, philosopher, professor, etc.); the Politician (senator, deputy, minister); the Adolescent (the child in the family, schoolboy, the lover, the artist, the soldier); the Idealist, Pierrot's grandchild in whiteface.

Can I be wrong? It seems to me there is a gold mine here, and something that no one can steal, imitate, or undo. It should take three years to prepare for this.[39]

Copeau gave his students the assignment of creating contemporary Commedia characters. They were asked to develop lazzi, to find the rhythms, walks, and personal gestures of these characters, and eventually to find a verbal phrase that belonged to their personage.[40] Students improvised Commedia-type scenarios. Although Copeau wrote and directed several plays based on Commedia types and plots, his work did not spark a general interest in reviving this form.[41] The renewal of the theater he hoped would be engendered by the rediscovery of the Commedia never came to pass.

The most technically demanding movement form to inspire Copeau was the Japanese Noh. Here, allegorical characters provided the concept of symbolic gesture, the physical abstraction of an idea.[42] Despite precision of corporal expresion implicit in the Noh, its staid and controlled form seems to be the antithesis of the primitive and natural gesture Copeau appeared to be seeking in other movement work. André Gide comments on this point:

> He [Copeau] terrifies me when he declares that he was never so near the attainment of his goal than in the Japanese Noh which he staged. . . . A play with no relation to our traditions, our customs, our beliefs, the exactitude of which was absolutely unverifiable, totally factitious, made up of slowness, pauses, something indefinably strained toward the supernatural in the tone of voice, gestures, and expressions of the actors.[43]

In fact, Copeau's obsession with the Noh elucidates his goals. Copeau was fundamentally a classicist. His new methods were not meant to be a substitute for ancient techniques, but a means of rediscovering their essential qualities, a way of taking theater back to its origins. Unlike other directors of the avant-garde, he was not interested in new scenic techniques that would remove the mise-en-scène from the text. He wished to reveal the essence of the classic texts. He believed that providing his actors with proper training would give them the technique necessary for this unveiling of the classics in their original form. As such, the Noh was the ideal form to reveal the epitome of technical development within the demands of the ancient tradition. All of Copeau's innovative ideas grew out of a respect for the past.

The Vieux-Colombier fostered a new concept of the actor. Copeau's students developed a physical awareness and discipline never before demanded in a French acting school. Despite this major thrust in the training, the *jeu physique* of the actor was considered only a preparation for revitalizing the traditional spoken theater. As such, many of the great names in the succeeding generation of French theater link back to Copeau—Charles Dullin, Louis Jouvet, Jean Dasté, and Michel Saint-Denis.[44] What is most significant for the purposes of this book is that all four men responsible for the renaissance of mime trace their heritage directly back to Copeau and the Vieux-Colombier.

GENEALOGY OF MODERN FRENCH MIME

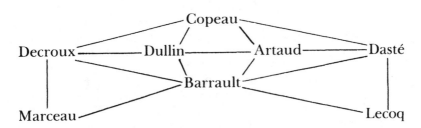

If the new mime traces its ascendance back to a school for dramatic actors, must it now be considered a theatrical mime? The analysis of the Copeau training, with its emphasis on acrobatics, circus, Commedia, Noh, and other mask work, indicates that although the ultimate goal was to produce a versatile dramatic actor, the means was a resuscitation and synthesis of all the elements of the mime tradition. If anything, Copeau brought to life a dying art; it is therefore not at all startling that all the contemporary French mimes trace their origins to his work. Copeau actually provided the missing link between contemporary aesthetics and the ancient mime tradition.

Nonetheless, it remains that the new mime was born in a formal acting school whose program was based on a well-conceived ideology of the theater. Such philosophic orientation was representative of the era itself; the time of upheaval of the old political order in Europe, the dawn of applied Marxism, the generation of Freud, the moment of modern science, the epoch of relativism. The new mime is a child of the times, the era Barrault calls "the golden age of aesthetics."[45]

The conscious theorizing of that time engendered a search for new forms. As Copeau had succeeded in integrating various theatrical traditions, Antonin Artaud, through the bizarre workings of his mind, synthesized the prevalent ideologies: elements of surrealism, symbolism, psychology, and cultural anthropology appear in his writings. His words are the summation of Copeau's views on corporeal expression in the theater and are echoed throughout the contemporary mime movement.

> I say that the stage is a concrete physical place which asks to be filled and to be given its own concrete language to speak. . . . that this concrete language to which I refer is truly theatrical only to the degree that the thoughts it expresses are beyond the reach of the spoken language. . . . It permits the substitution, for the poetry of language, of a poetry in space. . . . One form of this poetry in space belongs to sign language . . . a language of signs, gestures and attitudes having an ideographic value as they exist in certain unperverted pantomimes.
>
> By "unperverted pantomime" I mean direct pantomime where gestures—instead of representing words or sentences as in our European Pantomime which is merely a distortion of the mute roles of Italian comedy—represent ideas, attitudes of mind, aspects of nature. . . .
>
> This language which evokes in the mind images of an intense natural (or spiritual) poetry provides a good idea of what a poetry in space independent of spoken language could mean in the theatre.[46]

Artaud, whose contribution is discussed later, took Copeau's ideas, applied them to mime and gave a call to action—a call that was received. This rejection of the nineteenth-century pantomime form with its literal replication of reality is repeated by each of the four proponents of a new mime form.

3

ETIENNE DECROUX
(1898–   )

Etienne Decroux—the creator of the modern mime form—
made his first contact with the theater in 1923, at the Ecole du
Vieux Colombier. A youthful anarchist, he joined the group of
nonactors in attendance there in the hope of improving his
political oratory. He was so inspired by the creative movement
work used by Copeau that he altered the direction of his life.

> If there hadn't been those exercises at the Vieux Colombier,
> probably I would have never chosen the path that I have.
> What did I do? I believed in the beauty of those exercises. I
> saw an artistic genre and I threw myself into it to add, and
> add, and add.[1]

When the school closed, Decroux continued in the theater,
working with Copeau's three protégés: Gaston Baty, Louis
Jouvet, and, at the Atelier, Charles Dullin and then later with
Antonin Artaud. But these men, like Copeau, were primarily
concerned with spoken theater and innovative textual interpretation. Still, Copeau's use of all the traditional mimetic techniques led Decroux to claim that modern mime "found its roots
at the Vieux Colombier."[2] Decroux began to envisage other
possible contexts for Copeau's training. He soon became the
advocate of a new silent mime, functioning independently of
traditional theater, and differing radically from the nineteenth-
century *pantomime blanche*. In an eightieth birthday interview,

Decroux stated that the idea for corporeal mime "came from the Vieux Colombier, all from the improvisations done with Jacques Copeau. I invented nothing. I invented only the belief in mime. That evidently is a lot!"[3] The more he worked, the more certain Decroux became that such an autonomous art was feasible. He quickly became a fanatic for the cause.

Decroux's corporeal mime is marked by a seriousness of purpose and self-conscious aesthetics that distinguishes it significantly from the old pantomime. This removes the new mime from the category of popular culture and renders it an experience for the intellectual elite. In generations past, when mime was a peoples' art, the primary concern was to entertain the masses, and no attention was paid to philosophic considerations. Decroux shifted the traditional emphasis, by constantly theorizing and caring little for the entertainment value of what he did.

> Pantomime: that play of face and hands which seemed to try to explain things but lacked the needed words. I detested this form. But that's rather strange because pantomime was always supposed to amuse people. I thought one could make a serious art form. Art should be serious first of all. . . . An art is first of all serious and adds the comic aspect later. And this pantomime seemed to me to be systematically comic, even before one knew what the subject was.[4]

The new seriousness brought concern for definition, codification, and categorization. Decroux was obsessed with developing a vocabulary and systematic technique that would establish the independence of mime from dance and theater; the new mime was to be an autonomous art.

In this spirit, Decroux, in 1928, organized a group of young actors interested in developing this art. Unfortunately his cohorts did not share his zealous devotion to the cause, and, after a series of disappointing efforts, Decroux "fell back on the only reliable elements, his wife and himself."[5] Together they presented a mime act, *La Vie Primitive* at the Salle Lancry in 1931. The performance received little notice, but Decroux was not discouraged. Later that year, Jean-Louis Barrault arrived at Dullin's Atelier where Decroux was working, and in him, Etienne Decroux had at last found "someone who was not only gifted, but also desired the presentation of mimes before the public."[6] Together they expanded *La Vie Primitive* and created a sequel—*La Vie Médiévale.*

Created from 1931 through 1940, *Primitive Life* showed man unrestrained by clothes and social conventions. The actor portrayed the happy savage, at ease in motion, most truly himself when rejoicing in the harmonious efforts of his muscles. This ideal found its source in the writings of Jean-Jacques Rousseau. Decroux's early vision of men from the Islands—Hawaii, Tahiti, and Samoa—all became one in the poet's mind. The activities of climbing a tree, picking a coconut, throwing it to his mate on the ground, shinnying down the tree, and rowing down a river, were represented by the actor.

Life of the Middle Ages (La Vie Médiévale), . . . again owes much to Rousseau, in particular his book *Emile,* in which Rousseau gives his ideal son the craft of carpenter. The carpenter is an artist, an athlete, an intellectual, a man who works with wood, with his heart and his head and his hands. This idea found an echo in Decroux's socialist temperament and in his work *The Carpenter.* The carpenter's wife is a worker, too, and her job is shown in *The Washing (The Washerwoman).* . . .[7]

Decroux continued working on ideas that were germinating in these pieces. *The Carpenter* and *The Washerwoman* have been used as work studies in economy and the manipulation of the object to the present.[8] A reworking of the original *Combat* performed with Barrault as part of *Primitive Life* was presented in 1945 at the Comedie Française as part of Shakespeare's *Antony and Cleopatra.*

Eric Bentley believes the *Combat Antique* to be perhaps "the most impressive of Decroux's compositions. . . ." for "Decoux has sought in the act of combat all possible shades of corporeal expression. . . ." The study "suggests how much dramatic substance there is during a fight even when 'nothing is going on' during the taking up of a stance (1), the holding of a blocked position (2), the momentary stop after a recoil (3), or the wait before a spring. . . ."[9]

Decroux and Barrault worked zealously to define the new mime, their successful collaboration ending in 1933, when Barrault was called into military service. Decroux's work with Barrault marked the beginning of a lifetime exploration of the mime form. Decroux's work has remained in a continual state of evolution. In fact, today, in his eighties, he is still searching for new techniques and styles of movement. His early work with Barrault was dedicated to definition and codification, the development of a technical base upon which to build an art form. The early technique was focused on what is now referred to as illusionary mime, a form Decroux was later to abandon as an end in and of itself. Decroux's concern became less with the creation of the illusion, and more with the spiritual ramifications of action and movement.

Decroux and Barrault underscored the distinction between the terms *mime* and *pantomime,* using the latter to refer to the old style, the former to the art they were to create. After centuries of interchanageability, the two words once again were to denote different forms. During their two years together, this duo did more to advance a systematized mime technique than had ever before been accomplished during the entire history of the art. They approached their work as a science, seeking to establish the basic principles of the craft. It was a most balanced collaboration; Barrault wrote,

> We complemented each other well. Decroux, through his strong analytic sense and exceptional creative intelligence, knew how to fix the improvised variations which I exercised more spontaneously than he.[10]

Decroux had been very much influenced by the extensive mask work done by Suzanne Bing at the Ecole du Vieux Colombier. He and Barrault did a great deal of their research masked, believing that the mask focuses attention on the body, magnifying movement, rendering it easier to "see the quality of what you're doing."[11] In order to permit total freedom and legibility of gesture, they worked in almost total nudity. They used no musical accompaniment, allowing nothing to detract from absolute corporal concentration.

The concept of the spinal column as the center of being was the point of departure for their theories.

> The man who walks has decided to move, and what he moves first is his center, that magic hollow box, thanks to which he breathes and is held up as an emblem of life, by that most supple staff in the world—his vertebral column.[12]

They worked on the idea of movement emanating from the spine, illustrating the point with activities as basic as walking; for Decroux viewed the simple act of walking as the first drama of man. It is the initial disequilibrium that puts him in peril and from which he must recover. The study of the recurrent loss of equilibrium in human activity is the study of dramatic movement. To walk, "the chest, via a supple spine, must express the desire to move, and it is under this will that the legs move."[13] The trunk of the body was established as the source of expression, with the limbs drawing upon its energy for all movement. They concluded: "It is the spine which gives gesture its dimension and style."[14]

The spine can only function as the source of movement if the body is supple, agile, and able to respond to the spine's directions. To this end, Decroux and Barrault developed a series of basic exercises that prepared the body for mime training; these entailed:

1. Exercise for total relaxation: equivalent of cleansing.
2. Awareness of isolated muscles, learning above all how to contract one muscle, leaving all the others relaxed.
3. Awareness of muscle groups.
4. Acquisition of muscle tone: neither contraction nor relaxation.
5. Development of abdominal muscles.
6. Scales around the spinal column.
7. Study of the spine as a whip.
8. Sincerity in sensation.
9. Development of concentration: Analytic concentration. Respiratory concentration. Wandering points of concentration.[15]

These progressively structured exercises were the basis from which Decroux's technique evolved. First, aspiring mimes must learn to ready the body through relaxation and mental surveillance and domination of the musculature, to purge themselves of all external preoccupations that can create tension. Steps two and three enable them to acquire precision of movement, which renders the mimic expression more articulate. Four and five yield flexibility and strength. Six and seven increase the range of spinal movement and, ergo, the range of expressive possibilities through exercises using the spine as the center of action. Eight links emotion to movement. Nine focuses energy.

The total process depends on mental images controlling a body rendered obedient by a carefully developed *gymnastique*. The student is now ready to learn the techniques of mime, techniques that were to be codified after scientific experimentation. Through their work, Decroux and Barrault developed a grammar of mime, a way to describe "a sentence of silence":

> I, the *subject,* is made up of the spinal column and the respiratory system. It is the torso. It is oneself. It is the silhouette. It is the *attitude.*
> The *verb* is the being in *movement.* It is the very action of the torso.
> The complement is created by the limbs. It is *indication.*
> This is how my body says a sentence of silence in space: Subject or attitude; verb or movement; complement or indication.[16]

The mime grammar enables the body to speak.

Decroux believes that mime is first of all a series of actions in the present tense. These actions must be executed with complete economy of movement, expending no more physical or emotional energy than absolutely necessary. If done correctly, the mime should be in a state of neutrality, imputing no meaning to his actions, for "the economical is without mannerism."[17] The performer at this early stage of training, learns to escape his own idiosyncratic gesture, as well as the tendency to artifically assume those of other characters. The *gymnastique* is the key to achieving economy and neutrality.

Decroux and Barrault's most important contribution to mime technique was the formulation of the *contrepoids* concept, a means for creating illusion in modern mime.

By the time their brief collaboration ended, the work involved in establishing the basic principles of mime had advanced a long way. Unfortunately Decroux could find no adequate replacement for Jean-Louis Barrault who was to follow a different road in the theater; thus Decroux was obliged to continue his research alone.

During the years that followed, Decroux acted in a variety of roles in the Paris theater, while in his spare time he continued work on a further elucidation of his mime theories. In order to perfect his technique, he gave hundreds of private performances to audiences that were often as small as two people. In 1941, when he felt he had sufficiently clarified his theories and crystalized the abstract principles into a practicable technique, he opened a school of mime in Paris.

Much of the Decroux technique as it evolved was an expansion of the earlier research with Barrault, although the focus shifted from illusionary mime to more abstract forms of corporeal expression. The early technique centered on three concepts: *l'attitude, le contrepoids,* and *le raccourci.*

Jean Dorcy, the noted mime and dance critic, who had known Decroux from their days together at the Vieux Colombier, believed the *raccourci* and the *contrepoids* to be the keys to the Decroux technique in the 1940s. The *contrepoids,* a concept developed in the early stages of Decroux's work, is defined as a tangible muscular compensation for intangible imaginary forces. "The imaginary existence of an object will become real when the body of the mime appropriately expresses the muscular perturbation that this object imposes upon it."[18]

> When we carry a bucket of water, what happens? In order to re-establish the equilibrium interrupted by the weight of the water, the free arm, in muscular response, stretches and contracts. If we take away the bucket while still desiring to suggest its existence, this muscular response, far from disappearing, must be accentuated. The system of muscular reaction conditioned by effort is the *contrepoids* of Etienne Decroux.[19]

The *contrepoids* is the basis for modern mime's ability to conjure the existence of the intangible. As Decroux's technique evolved, the *contrepoids* referred to the emotional weight of an action as well. *The contrepoids* is a technique that can be taught along with other mime exercises. The *raccourci,* however, is not that simply defined, and requires a unique talent to perform it.

The word *raccourci* literally means a foreshortening, but this is "evidently not a lessening, shrinking, or stylization. It is the condensation of an idea in space and time."[20] If the mime is to achieve this "broad synthesis"[21] of thought in movement, he must first abstract the essence of a particular movement; e.g., running, climbing, swimming. He must then compress the action into its essential parts, still keeping it comprehensible and recognizable. He is thus expressing an action without actually performing it. It is this technique that enables the mime to give the illusion of performing certain acts, such as walking long distances or climbing, while remaining in place. He is able to suggest the action to the audience through its condensation into its physical and psychological primary components. Later Decroux often referred to this technique as simplification and amplification. The *raccourci* is an optical illusion, a *trompe l'oeil*, comprising gesture and emotion.

The *raccourci* is the key to abstraction in Decroux's art, for it is evocative of certain movements without rendering them literally. Still, the *raccourci* depends on an identification of the action alluded to by the foreshortened gesture, and as such, is neither totally abstract nor symbolic. The combined use of the *raccourci*, which evokes certain recognizable movements, with the *contrepoids*, which conjures up the presence of invisible elements of reality, yields the illusion of the tangible world. Decroux's early art thus presented a stylization of reality.

Using the *contrepoids* and the *raccourci*, Decroux developed a codified definitional system that gave gestural equivalents to certain verbs: to walk, to climb, to pull, to skate, and so on. During this period, Decroux used no props, as his art depended upon the successful creation of illusion. The illusion was sustained by the implementation of the *contrepoids* and the *raccourci*. Later, as the emphasis on illusionary mime lessened, props were integrated into many pieces.

Decroux, influenced by Delsarte, explored positions that would reflect certain interior emotional states: fear, anger, love, or bliss for example. He discovered that subtle changes in spinal position or muscle tone would create an exterior manifestation of age or sentiment. Decroux's goal was the development of a vocabulary of set legible movements that would be easily transmissible from master mime to student as are the positions of classical dance. This comprehensive and systematic technique would differ radically from the old pantomime and ancient mime, which had no fixed aesthetics. Decroux believed mime remained a marginal art for this very reason and that his codified mime grammar would enable mime to attain the autonomy and recognition accorded dance.

The manner of codification is explained by Barrault, who tells of the three weeks it took to codify the famous *marche sur place* (creation of the illusion of walking distances while remaining in place), through experimenting with the arrangement of disequilibriums, *contrepoids*, respiration, and isolation of energy, until the desired effect of the *raccourci* was attained.[22]

The concept of *l'attitude* is less easily defined. Its actual role in

the Decroux tehnique is a difficult one to grasp, and even Decroux's own explanations do little to elucidate its meaning: "Attitude is the punctuation of mime," he says, "and it follows that
it is not its substance. . . . Attitude is more than the punctuation
of movement, it is its witness . . . one can conceive of movement
as a series of attitudes."[23] It is as if each frame of a motion-
picture film revealed not just a pose, but a dimension of style
and meaning beyond gesture. Thus *l'attitude* expresses both
pose and mood. The formulation of *l'attitude* reflects the influence of oriental theater, where pose is emphasized.

Since "the mime does not produce presences recognizable as
conventional signs"[24] in modern pantomime, he must add
another dimension to his work. The expression of this through
a physical posture assumed during movement is *l'attitude* and as
such is the source of all meaning beyond the literal. Thus, any
modification of economic movement in order to express an
idea, emotion, or a characterization is the use of *l'attitude*.

Through *l'attitude* the audience not only recognizes parts of
the movement, but also the state of mind that would normally
accompany a particular action, and is thus able to identify the
verb of the movement. The *raccourci* depends upon *l'attitude*.

> In playing a film in slow motion, one would normally see a
> slowing down of fragments of reality. But slow motion of
> modern mime should reveal gesture in which many others
> were synthesized.[25]

Alvin Epstein, a Decroux disciple, breaks down the components of movement in another way, yet he still describes it as
moving from economy to attitude and style: All movement can
be analyzed in terms of "design, rhythm, and intensity. . . . The
design of a movement is of course its trajectory through space
. . . creating a rhythm within our movement by the varying
lapses of time between points in our path."[26] Intensity is determined by the degree of relaxation and tension with which we
perform the movement, and it allows for many variations. All
deviations from the economical use of design, rhythm, and
intensity will give an emotional texture to the mime content.
The selective emphasis upon any or all of the "basic qualities"[27]
of movement emanating from an inner energy source is what
Decroux would call *l'attitude*. It is thus the basis of all characterization, as well as the substance of content. It is the vehicle

through which the mime can allude to multifaceted interpretations. It is possible to perform the same design of movement in various ways, changing its meaning only through the alteration of rhythm and intensity.

Using their original idea of the spine as the center of being, Decroux and Barrault established a hierarchy of expressive organs: The torso first, then legs and arms, hands and feet, and last of all, the face. "The trunk can be all the body," writes Decroux, "as long as the arms and legs move only at the command of the torso, as a projection of its line of force."[28] He explains:

> The trunk is there as a counterweight and for emotional expression.
> Arms are made to seize and convert the direction of the body's bulk.
> Legs were made to come and go, as it is in walking that one best expresses character.
> The head is made for perception.
> One must use the face with moderation, and renounce the expression of soul states with the arms.
> Remember my satiric verse:
> "It is the trunk that suffers while the arms complain."[29]

Decroux talks of shock and resonance: the reverberation throughout the body of the initial impulse felt by the torso.

Believing the face to be the least essential source of physical expression, Decroux continued the extensive use of masks.

> One may be sublime with a mask, but not with a face. The face has something incurably realistic about it. It's there! But we change the body easily, because the body is made up of large parts. And the moment a large enough stick moves, everyone sees it. The face, however, is made of smaller units, and it's truly difficult to transfigure it. But the mask transfigures it.[30]

The face represents the self that the actor must leave behind. Decroux conceives of the new mime as being antirealistic, and therefore he desires to "liberate the actor from the fatality of his own face."[31]

Thus the mask has two bases in the Decroux technique: First, it emphasizes the action of the body, thereby forcing the audience to focus on corporeal expression; second, it creates a degree of abstraction that removes mime from the literal realistic plane and temporarily separates the mime himself from his own identity, permitting him to portray types different from his own character or sex. The mask increases the range of expressive possibilities.

Decroux states, "The mask is a socialist invention."[32] Here we perceive echoes of the young anarchist who was first fascinated by Copeau's mask exercises. But the mask means more than an equalizing of potential to Decroux, who believes that the denial of the individual's identity removes mime from the hold of psychological realism.

> Thanks to the mask, we'd see that dramatic art can join other art forms.
> When one looks at a sculptor, one sees that he does not resemble his work. . . . The subject distinguishes itself from the object. . . .
> So, thanks to the mask, the dramatic actor can work more in the way of the poet, the sculptor, the painter, the designer. The mask permits not only justice, since justice is not universally respected, but it permits use of talent that otherwise would be lost, talent like gold hidden in the earth, or like a little child lost in the ocean.[33]

Mime, born out of the rebellion against naturalism initiated by Copeau, was urged toward abstract form by Decroux. To this end, Decroux experimented with a variety of different masks. Among these he preferred the veiled face, created by pulling a translucent fabric taut over the face and chin, revealing only the outline of the features. The cloth was tied at the back of the head; no excess material hung below the neck. Decroux appreciated the neutral expressionless qualities of this mask. He explains:

> What do I mean by the term neutral or inexpressive mask? The neutral or inexpressive mask has a form that permits the actor to portray all possible sentiments without being ridiculous. Thanks to the neutrality of the mask I can depict joy by jumping in the air, or anger by jumping in the air, without anyone finding a dissonance between the mask and what I'm doing. I could depict repose, or the need for activity, dying, or sleeping, or waking up. If this mask allows me to do every-

thing, even the most diverse and contradictory things, without seeming ridiculous, then it's a neutral mask.[34]

The harmony between the actor and the mask is a primary goal of mime. The veil facilitates this compatibility, as it expresses no emotion.

Use of the veil creates an element of stylization visible in other visual arts:

> To stylize in sculpture, you use bumps or hollows. Either you add clay and it's a bump, or you take away clay and it's a hollow. But in making a mask, I can take away only a little clay. I can make a small hollow only. We can't hollow out the actor's flesh. We can add, but not take away. We're condemned to have a mask larger than we want. The more I stylize, the more I add, since I can't take away. The head will consequently get larger.[35]

The veil enables Decroux to mask the face without increasing the size of the head. Therefore, compared to more traditional masks, the veil is less distracting, and accomplished the desired degree of abstraction.[36]

Decroux used the veil in *Les Arbres,* where the mime evokes the image of trees. Here the veil serves to blend the face with the body, camouflaging the persistently human head, without distracting from the action, and allowing the body totality to become a metaphor for the tree.

Decroux's sensitivity to contemporary aesthetic theory in the plastic arts is evidenced by the various abstract masks he devised.[37] Cubism affected his work most directly.[38]

> Suppose you had made the perfect mask in clay. You could reduce the curves of that face to facets, to prism-like surfaces, so that the smallest movement of the head would reflect light from one of the facets. Wearing a mask like this is like turning on the light. You put on such a mask to see the quality of corporeal movement.[39]

The concept of form and texture giving meaning and tone through the mask is expressed by Decroux:

> There's another mask, one made contrary to the faceted one, with parts rounder than our real faces are. This kind of mask

wouldn't have the advantage of the faceted mask, but it would have a contrary advantage. It would have the poetic quality of retrospective understanding.[40]

The mask, for Decroux, was thus radically different in form and function from its predecessors. The earlier mimes and pantomimists used masks that expressed human stereotypes or archetypes.[41] But Decroux sees the mask as a means of camouflaging the performer, liberating him to be other than what he is. The mask uses form to facilitate evocative non-naturalistic movement.

Decroux's mask theory was very much influenced by Gordon Craig, whom he cites as a primary source of the new mime.[42] Craig decried the imperfection of the human form as an expression of thought, for he believed in symbolic gesture executed by an actor in complete control of his physical and emotional being, and thus unfettered by the chains of psychological realism.[43] Craig believed this pefect actor did not and could not exist.

> There has never been an actor who has so trained his body from head to foot that it would answer to the workings of his mind without permitting the emotions even so much as to awaken. . . . never, never: there never has been an actor who reached such a state of mechanical perfection that his body was absolutely the slave of his mind.[44]

Craig thus proffered the substitution of the marionette for the actor, as a marionette is free from a psychological past and binding identity. It can manifest visually the pure expression of thought without emotional interference or physiological limitation.

Decroux applauded Craig's ideas,[45] and adapted them to his view of mime: "If the marionette is the image of the ideal actor, one should attempt to acquire the virtues of the ideal marionette."[46] He set out to form a human marionette—the modern mime: First Decroux masked the face, the key to the individual's identity and emotional past that must be left behind; now, the mime must transform his body into a totally pliable instrument, capable of acting out the directives of thought. For this, Decroux established the *gymnastique dramatique*.

Using the nine basic mime exercises enumerated earlier, the

actor develops muscular awareness, plasticity, flexibility, and control. He broadens his range of movement through the expansion of his physical potential. The development of the body into a totally controlled instrument of expression (like the marionette) is the goal of Decroux's training.

> What I have done is to consider the human body as a keyboard—the keyboard of a piano. Of course this is only an analogy. We know that the human body cannot be exactly like a keyboard. On a keyboard we can always isolate one note from another, but we can't isolate the chest from the head. If the chest moves, the head automatically does something. But nevertheless, the thought is there. . . . So we consider the keyboard as something that should inspire us. Nothing should happen in the body except what is desired and calculated. The actor should bear the relationship to his body that a pianist does to the keyboard. And to him who says, "Isn't that a little dry? Where is the fantasy, the temperament, the genius?" I would reply humorously, "Do you think music has no fantasy? Do you think music has no genius?"
>
> Music seems to paint the most accurate portrait of our moods. It seems that music is never betrayed by anything. No one has ever said that was dry. That would be a joke! Many people consider music to be the most exciting art form, greatest of the arts. And yet it's the most technical art. A musician doesn't do just anything. Everything is calculated. The human body should follow the example of the instrumentalist. He should say, "My body will be like the keyboard, and what I plan to do will be like solfège, like notes."[47]

The keyboard is analagous to the marionette principle of Craig. The process by which the body attains this control is the *gymnastique.*

The keyboard analogy is reflected in the isolation exercises so fundamental to the Decroux training. To promote muscular awareness and control, physical movement is divided into inclination, rotation, and translation. Any unit of the body may move in these three manners. Using different parts of the body in different ways, combinations and permutations of these movements are possible. The mime learns to separate the head from the neck, the neck from the chest, chest from the waist, waist from the pelvis, etc. This ability to isolate units of the body ultimately gives expressive control and greater range of movement possibilities. It creates a degree of physical articulation that separates Decroux's mime from the pantomime of other eras. It has also resulted in an angularity and degree of stylization that distinguishes the Decroux-trained mime from other performers.

Eric Bentley, upon seeing Decroux demonstrate his isolation exercises reflected on the process:

> In his [Decroux's] presence one has no doubt that all that occurs is important. Even technical exercises. Decroux showed us how he makes each part of the body progressively more independent of the others: we glimpsed the ubermarionette in the process of creation.[48]

In his search to find *le mime subjectif,* a mime free of narrative context, capable of multiple interpretations, Decroux created *le mime statuaire,* for "mime is most real when, like sculpture, it contains the properties of what it depicts: resistance, breakability, weight and volume."[49] Decroux explains the influence of statuary art on his work:

> My passion, my zeal for mime . . . grew out of my fervor for sculpture and its sensual, carnal pleasure, which inspired me even as a child . . . I had the confirmed ambition of finding a style of mobile sculpture outside of the dance. It was, in the end, the teachings at the Vieux Colombier, where the mask and the naked body were of prime importance, that inspired me to see their role in dramatic creation."[50]

The new tradition was founded out of this sculptural concept. Decroux decided that henceforth

> The old pantomime is dead; the pantomime as one performed it in days gone by—anecdotal, chatty, burdened by futile traditions, and subordinated to an alphabet, an all too formal code. The mobile statuary mime bears it so little resemblance that it actually constitutes a new art, a modern art.[51]

In formulating the philosophy of *le mime statuaire* the preeminence of the torso emerges again, for it is this emphasis placed upon the dominant expressive qualities of the torso in the new mime technique that gives it its intrinsic link to the sculptural *integritas* for which Decroux strives. Rodin made the observation that Michelangelo's sculpture "could be rolled downhill without any essential part being broken off."[52] In such an experiment, the extremities would of course be the first parts to break, yet the essential significance of the work would remain intact, as the source of its expression lies within the lines of the trunk of the body. The mime, like the sculptor, must therefore seek to establish the emotional elements of his subject within both the physical and spiritual center of his being (the torso), allowing the limbs to resound the central feeling and posture. It is the expressive force of the trunk that allows us to perceive the subject and action of Greek and Roman sculpture despite lost limbs.

Le mime statuaire differed dramatically from the *pantomime blanche* and earlier mime forms.

> Statuary mime, rather than attempting to combine movement with dialogue, music, or song in a seemingly improvised and spontaneous art as in the Commedia dell'Arte, depicts arrested, imaginative, significant movement in silence, like a Rodin statue, motionless yet bursting with potential movement. Instead of breaking forth into facile movement, statuary mime gradually evolves from movement into immobility, seeking to stir the imagination by suggestion.[53]

"Total use of the body in the new mime replaced the physical bias of the old pantomime, which played upon two chords—explanatory hand movements and facial expression."[54] For hand and face gesture are most often literal. The old pantomime was a system of conventional gestures for which the performer needed only to learn the signs. The vocabulary was passed on from one generation to the next. Of course, the great mimes, such as Deburau, injected a great deal of creativity into the arrangement of the conventional gestures, as well as personal verve to the performance. But they were fundamentally dealing with narrative forms that were easily recognizable by their public. The *pantomime blanche* told a story in a language similar to that used by deaf mutes, therefore emphasizing hand or facial movements as opposed to use of the total expressive range of the body. The new mime tries to establish a more flexible definition system, with multiple interpretations possible. It is a subjective art, as unique as the performer can make it and as personal as the spectator cares to take it. "With the new mime we no longer read known forms, but decipher, reconstitute, and appreciate according to our ability and emotional state."[55] The contemporary audience demands an active interpretive role in an art form not limited by reality and capable of symbolic meaning. The stage is thus stripped bare of all the accoutrements of realism, leaving only the visual images of the body in space to create meaning.

To emphasize the sculptural quality of the human body, Decroux often performed in a minimal loincloth that barely covered the genitals. He believed this physical exposure revealed the quality of movement. In the 1940s, he began performing in tights, sensing that this was perhaps less distracting, yet still could achieve the desired effect of the uncluttered line. Often the tights had hoods that covered the head—on which a mask was worn; thus no part of the body was revealed. He also appliquéd a white line onto black tights in such a way as to outline the human silhouette. When performing against a black backdrop, all that was visible was the white outline of a masked character—the sculptural abstraction of the human form. The new mime functions much as modern art, creating an image through points, lines, surfaces, and colors.

The concept of symbolic gesture is evidenced in the theories of Craig and Artaud and indicates that Decroux was sensitive to the prevalent theatrical ideologies. At its best, Decroux's mime appears to be imagistic, impressionistic, and evocative. Nevertheless, Decroux's efforts often succumb to the anecdote he strains to avoid.

A question of interest in any analysis of Decroux's work must be the issue of emotional and internal connection to the external movement. There is little doubt that Decroux himself experiences such a connection in his own work. In his later technique, he clearly intended the counterweight to refer to the emotional, as well as the physical, weight of an action. He believed that when the body is pushed, the emotional link is inevitable, that the force of the body creates an energy. But Decroux's technique itself does not teach the mime how to find this vital link to his internal self. Many of Decroux's students appear to be copying the line of the movement, but the action often appears empty. Yves Lebreton, a recent student of Decroux's confirms this: "I often see more 'engagement' and truth in a simple head turn of an old traditional actor late in his career than in all the statuary mime of a Decroux student."[56]

Lebreton talks of how rarely Decroux speaks of the internal

life of an actor. Instead he uses images of sap rising up through the body, filling the limbs.[57] But such images are often not enough to facilitate emotional connection. Decroux spends little time on the technique of respiratory links to movement that are the keys to connecting to internal sources.[58] It is Barrault who ultimately makes this synthesis.

Decroux, although not concerned with psychological character, is interested in the study of archetypes. He created categories for study, most prominently *homme des isles, homme de songe, homme de salon, homme de sport*. These require different combinations of line rhythm and intensity to create the appropriate personnage, i.e., the rhythm of the man of the islands would be slower than that of the man of the salon; the intensity of the man of sport different from the man of dreams. In these archetypes, Decroux is not seeking individual characterization, but universals.[59] It is a search for dominant sentiments and traits that can be crystallized in movement terms.

Decroux's attempts to distinguish between mime and dance elucidate his theories further. He believes mime could be arhythmic if it so chose, whereas dance is obligatorily rhythmic and is usually dependent on the timing imposed by a musical score. Mime's dramatic qualities often require that it upset rhythm for effect. Refusing any externally imposed tempo, Decroux allowed no musical accompaniment to mime until late in his career when he permitted the integration of sound and music with mime. He further differentiates between the two arts:

> The art of the dance, especially of the classical dance, is more painful than the art of mime, because the dancer goes beyond his needs. . . . He translates the natural movements of instinctive dance into anti-natural ones, therefore he suffers. The mime suffers to make us believe he suffers.[60]

This comment by Decroux demonstrates his concern for emotional content.

"Decroux emphasizes that his action is 'horizontal' whereas that of dance is 'vertical'."[61] What Decroux means is that mime uses the forces present in man's natural environment, whereas dance, on the other hand, attempts to defy the constraints of gravity, and through leaps and turns, enables man to enter another world beyond the natural one in which he lives. Decroux reiterates: "Mime, as I understand it, is Promethean, and I oppose it to dance in this way."[62] The impulse of mime is downward; its concerns concrete.

In an interview with Eric Bentley, Decroux explicates further:

> The dancer deals in symmetrical patterns, exact repetitions, regular rhythms, as music enjoins; the mime in asymmetry, variation, syncopation, the rhythmic patterns of speech and natural body movement. Dance comes from excess energy. . . . Pantomime is the energy it takes to turn the waterwheel; dance is the gay spectacular splash of the excess - water. . . . Watch dancers on the stage pretending to carry a grand piano. They rejoice in the hollowness of the pretense. They trip along. The piano has no weight. Now watch mimes going through the same act. They present precisely the weight of the piano by indicating the strain it occasions.[63]

Decroux is saying that the use of the *contrepoids*, physically and emotionally distinguishes mime from dance. It also ties mime to the tangible world. Decroux believes that mime can and should escape the confines of realism through the rendering of the spiritual via the physical. The question remains—can mime escape the forms and images of reality?

Dance critic Roger Garaudy believes it cannot, for whereas dance must "render visible the invisible,"[64] the mime must do just the opposite.

> Mime, by its very definition, is composed of movements representative of an already existent reality or concept. . . . The gesture of the mime is descriptive, that of dance is projective. . . . There exists between mime and the dance the same difference as between the concept which sums up what already exists and the myth that surpasses it.[65]

Decroux believes that his mime can escape the need to find reference points in reality, and indeed, as his mime grew increasingly abstract, he used fewer allusions. Much of his work is imagistic, a form of poetic realism. This description of *Les Arbres* is indicative of Decroux's use of concrete images to express poetic meaning.

> In *Les Arbres,* four mimes clothed in grey, bodies bent over, wearing veils to cover their faces, portray a cluster of trees.

As the trees free themselves from the earth, the mimes'
bodies slowly arise and sprout fingers through the inner life
of their trunks.[66]

The movements in this number were poetic and evocative, yet
still referred to an existing element of reality. Decroux's mime
appears here to be more impressionistic than abstract. In later
pieces such as *Meditation*, Decroux gives physical form to pure
thought, and succeeds in evoking the universal through the
concrete. It was not until late in his life, in the early 1960s, that
he created a number which is totally nonrepresentational—
even free of the human form: In *L'enveloppe*, where a billowing
drape totally camouflages the human body; all that appears are
the movements of an abstract form changing the shape of the
drape.

Today, Decroux's mime is moving more in this direction. As
the degree of abstraction grows within the mime form, while
modern dance becomes increasingly more earthbound, the
boundary between mime and dance becomes increasingly
difficult to define.

Just as he insisted on the independence of mime from dance,
Etienne Decroux, as the "apostle of silence,"[67] took a consist-
ently rigid position on the boundaries between mime and the
theater. He admitted that mime and the spoken word could be
combined in the theater, but only to their mutual detriment:
when used together they serve only as complements, neither
one sufficient unto itself. "One can therefore combine words
with pantomime on the condition that they are both impover-
ished . . . when two arts are produced together, one must with-
draw when the other advances."[68] Decroux sought the emancipation of the actor from the word. "When an actor speaks, he
shares the responsibility for his performances with the author
of his words; in fact, he becomes the author's slave."[69] The
tenacity with which Decroux clung to this position probably cost
him the collaboration of his great disciple Jean-Louis Barrault,
who believed in the fruitful marriage of mime and spoken theater.

Bentley provides an interesting analysis of Decroux's "pur-
ism."

Compare Decroux with Charlie Chaplin. . . . Why pantomime? The answer for Chaplin was: Because pantomime

was unmistakably called for—the motion picture was invented and the sound track was not. To be silent on principle, like the new French school of pantomime headed by Decroux is quite another matter . . . while for Chaplin a great deal was given by the situation, for Decroux all too much is imposed by the will and the intellect. . . . Decroux is at too many points retrenchment, retreat, abstention, rejection. The basis of such a theatre is highly theoretical, not to say precious.[70]

Decroux's stand was under constant fire from established theater people who believed mime was a dramatic art. Gaston Baty had this to say in an open letter to Decroux:

When Decroux tries to isolate mime, out of his love for it, from the rest of dramatic technique, he once more mutilates a major art at the expense of an in-spite-of-everything minor manifestation. It is an amputation that does not even present to us the body minus the limb, but, instead, only the limb, that has been amputated.[71]

The noted critic Hubert Engelhard comments:

I do not hesitate to affirm that the mime, in its purest form, is not, and doubtlessly has never been, a means of expression that comes naturally to man. . . . One has the constant impression while watching these actors [Decroux's], that they must perform acts of violence to themselves in order to prevent a cry or an exclamation from escaping. . . . I remain tied to a far too intellectual comprehension of the work, which must therefore be degenerated from the rest of theatrical art.[72]

Decroux remained undaunted by his critics, attributing their commentary to a lack of comprehension of his work. He continued decrying realism, aiming at symbolic gesture, while the critics maintained he was too literal. The commentaries on Decroux's performance indicate that the critics believed he never broke out of a limiting form: "'The Factory,' 'a symbolic chorus,' says the program, but in reality it is only a sort of drama in several acts."[73]

"La Sorcière," and "The Invisible Man," are only carnival parades and nothing more. . . . "The Factory," which is composed of several surprising inventions, creates no illusion. We remain on the earth, the earth of men.[74]

". . . in this enterprise there are borrowings from dance and from the literal realism of our routine theatre."[75] "The Gangster,' 'The City,' or 'Ice becomes Fire,' are formless and ordinary despite effective movement."[76] The critical commentary suggests that Decroux, who so strongly desired to elevate the art of mime from the narrative, literal pantomime of the past to a universal, symbolic, evocative art, often did not succeed in this intention.

If the critical reaction is correct, it is clear that Decroux is a less-than-successful performer. Those who review his work do so with sincere deference to the great contribution he has made in the establishment of both a mime technique and a pedagogical approach through which the craft can be taught. Decroux is lauded as a teacher and politely censured for his inability to make contact with an audience. Jean Dorcy, who was once Decroux's teacher and later a friend, and critic for over fifty years, put it this way:

Decroux was hostile towards those he should have seduced. He did not like his public; worse than that, he had only disdain for them. It is said he even took a malicious pleasure in irritating them.[77]

Barrault confirms:

When we were doing public performances of our mime numbers, if Decroux ever lost his balance, he would begin the whole act again from the beginning. The audience would then break into laughter. Decroux would stop again, walk towards the audience and insult them, shouting how they understood nothing about the artist's pain.[78]

and Engelhard reiterates:

There is no doubt that Etienne Decroux refuses to make any concession to his audience. . . . The entire distance between our world and his—the spectator must go it alone.[79]

When Decroux came to America between 1959 and 1961, the American press was properly reverent. Yet nowhere can one find a rave review of his performances. Instead, polite excuses were made for his failure as a performer, while the critics made the inevitable comparisons with Marceau, who had already won the admiration of the American public. From the *New York Times:*

> People for whom the art is represented by Marcel Marceau (a former pupil of Decroux's) will find the show at the Cricket less theatrical, less bravura, and more intellectual than anything M. Marceau has brought to this country. Marceau's mime-theatre; Decroux's mime-concert.[80]

The *New York World Telegram and Sun:* "Perhaps Marceau has spoiled us. His pantomime is subtle and refined. The mime theatre of Etienne Decroux by contrast is explicit, exaggerated and gross."[81]

There seemed to be an acknowledgment of the pedagogical significance of Decroux's work despite his inability to perform. From *Variety:* "A pantomimist is an orator who talks to the world, and a mime is an actor who speaks to other actors. An orator cannot turn his back on the audience. A mime can and does."[82] The New York Post: "His own solos are more of a demonstration."[83] The *Herald Tribune:* "M. Decroux is not an incompetent. He is a teacher. . . . It is the teacher's fate never to be incomparable himself; he frees talent to go where he cannot."[84]

The critical commentary on his performances indicates the paradox of the theory and work of Etienne Decroux. An actor dedicates himself to the establishment of a fully detailed mime technique, one that will effectively establish it as an autonomous contemporary art form. He seeks to convince the world that such a performing art exists and then proceeds to consciously insult and ignore his audience, thereby contradicting the very nature of the art. Why would a man deliberately thwart the acceptance of his life's work?

Decroux, in a recent interview provides an answer to this question:

> I've been more concerned—and I'll finish with this—more concerned about making an art than concerned with showing off genius, or even showing off my talent. I'm not terribly interested in performing. It's not terribly important to me for someone to tell me I'm an extraordinary mime. I was talented, even so. That doesn't interest me. Genius fades. Art is eternal.[85]

Decroux's conviction that his primary mission was the creation of a new transmissible art form is verified by his faithful students who believe he has done just that. They acknowledge his idiosyncracies, express various points of view on his failings, but uniformly respect and revere the man. It is perhaps to his students, who in the end will continue his legacy, that we should turn for the final analysis.

Because of the high level of technical proficiency necessary to perform Decroux's corporeal mime, many students who do not study long enough end up imitating Decroux's exercises without feeling free enough within the form to integrate them into their own personal style. The result according to Kari Margolis and Tony Brown, "appears as vacuous robotlike performances. The technique is confused with performance, and Figures—short mime choreography encompassing a basic principle of study are presented as performance pieces."[86] Yves Lebreton suggests that it is Decroux's irrefutable ability to demonstrate that allows "the hurried observer to believe his work is expressed in categorical and systematic schemas."[87] "After leaving Decroux," says Yves Marc, "we took hold of the basics and reinvested all that we had learned. There comes a time when one can no longer refer to a system which belongs to another person. This is not a betrayal. Decroux's technique belongs to a man who has fifty years of work behind him, and who has his own reason to envision the work in a particular manner. If one wants to understand his ideas, one must reaffirm them in his own way."[88]

Thomas Leabhart, former Decroux student, and founder and editor of *Mime Journal* credits Decroux with having developed a technique that "gives the artist a mastery of his body so he is free to express what he intends to, through a universal system of movement, so that any part of the body can move through any plane with any dynamic desired by the actor."[89]

Perhaps Decroux's work is best summed up by Yves Lebreton:

Behind what is explained lives all that is not. Between what is said and what is done, what is demonstrated and what is suggested, what is defined and what is undefined exist the many incertitudes that only experience can resolve. The training of Etienne Decroux is not a well-defined framework of scientific measurements. It is an organism comprising its internal correspondences, its unsuspected ramifications, its play of reflections and echos so difficult to localize. . . . Etienne Decroux proposes more than a technique, a system, or a method. He inspires the discovery of our thinking body, above all, he demands a work ethic, and provokes an experience on you, in you, by you, directed towards others.[90]

Despite the laudatory appraisals of his students, there remains something unsettling in Decroux's inability to seduce the public. Decroux certainly is aware that mime, even by his own definition, is a performing art, and as such exists not in aesthetic theory alone, but through the interaction with the audience. That Decroux is concerned with "making an art" is evident, but how could he have hoped to create the following through which art is made eternal without concern for the implementation of his new techniques in performance?

One can only guess at the answer to this enigma. Decroux is known as an eccentric, and it is possible he truly did not believe his public merited, or was capable of understanding his talents.[91] Though his students believe he is a gifted performer, perhaps, he was just a limited actor, although a great theoretician.

Decroux's self-conscious aesthetics came between him and his public. It became an alienating seriousness. Barrault recalls Decroux saying to him, "You understand, this is no longer possible. When you perform mime, one doesn't feel it is work."[92] That Decroux felt this to be a flaw reflects a lack of understanding of the performer-audience dynamic. The public does not come to see work, but its fruit. Decroux's view of himself as a crusader for a new art prevented him from ever feeling completely free in its expression. It is Decroux's fanaticism that engendered a rigidity from which he could not escape.

Considering the enormity of the accomplishment of this man, his faults must be pardoned. He has singlehandedly created an art form that has served as an inspiration to two generations of mimes. As Bentley remarks, "If fanatacism is evil, as the world goes it is a necessary evil; no point will ever get enough emphasis unless somebody has given it too much."[93] Decroux, the father of the modern mime form, has given others the tools to go where he could not.

The questions that Bentley posed after his first encounter with Decroux over thirty years ago, remain:

"What in the end was one to make of the man? A genius who talks a certain amount of nonsense? An eccentric who talks a great deal of sense? A hero of heresy, a fanatic of a true faith?"[94]

4

JEAN-LOUIS BARRAULT
(1910–   )

Charles Dullin's Atelier was the postlude to the Vieux Colombier movement. There the major figures in French theater pooled their creative energies, producing a synthesis of the current trends. Dullin, a member of Copeau's first company, and perhaps the most brilliant and eclectic of his protégés, established the Atelier as a studio for theatre research. It was thus natural that the twenty-year-old Jean-Louis Barrault should have sought the tutelage of Dullin, and chosen the Atelier as the arena for his theatrical debut.

During his years at the Atelier, Barrault worked with the three men who most influenced his artistic development; he recounts:

> It would be too simple to separate the influence of Dullin from that of Decroux or Artaud. There was no succession of influences; it all worked inside of me simultaneously. But at the Grenier,[1] I had an instinctive rapport with Artaud.[2]

From Copeau's protégé, Dullin, who "advocated Meyerhold and practiced Stanislavski,"[3] Barrault learned the traditions of the theater. Dullin's concern with plastic expression, his love of the Commedia and stylized performance, and above all, his respect for the text were to mark all of Barrault's future work. Decroux indoctrinated Barrault in the physical techniques of acting. And Artaud opened the vista of the metaphysical di-

77

mensions of the stage. Barrault's artistic self became a composite of these three forces.

In 1931, when Barrault first arrived at the Atelier, Decroux recognized his talents for corporal expression and at once enlisted him in the quest for the new mime. For two years they were inseparable. Their invaluable collaboration and devotion to the cause resulted in the mime theories discussed in the preceding chapter. Of their time together Barrault says: "Those were two wonderful years thanks to Decroux who initiated me in the art of gesture and gave me a passion for corporal expression."[4] This relationship was terminated in 1933 when Barrault was drafted into the army.

Upon completion of his one-year military service, Barrault returned to the theater. He felt "a need to translate into action the fascinating lessons he had learned from Decroux."[5] But Decroux did not feel the same compelling need. Barrault tells of their parting of the ways:

> One day, Decroux said: "Me, I only want to work before an audience of two or three people." Now, as for me, obviously my desire was to perform my work before the largest possible audience. Then Decroux said: "Everything you are doing is out of touch with the work. Most definitely you are only a whore and you're wasting your time." And so he banished me. But on many occasions since then we have found ourselves together, and each time we have gotten along well . . . and it was marvelous. . . . But he never wanted to collaborate with me for long, as we had such differing temperaments.[6]

While Decroux was oriented toward the establishment of a mime dictionary, "wanting to simplify and render comprehensible most concrete actions on the stage: how to swim, to run, to climb,"[7] providing corporal translations for certain verbs and nouns, Barrault felt, "I'll get nowhere in life as a codifier, paper and pencil in hand. I act. I am a motorized being."[8] More recently, Barrault reiterates, "Decroux had a taste for writing and making a manual of the perfect mime, but I was more whimsical and unrestrained."[9] And so their conflicting personalities sent Decroux and Barrault down divergent paths. Yet each in his own way remained faithful to the basic principles of the new mime.

During the years that Barrault was at the Atelier, the major influences on his formative period were Decroux and Dullin.

Antonin Artaud had begun to share his ideas with the young Barrault, but it was not until the time of Grenier des Grands Augustins (an experimental group led by Barrault from 1936 to 1939) that their friendship, as well as their creative relationship, truly blossomed. They began to see each other on a daily basis. During these meetings, Artaud revealed his revolutionary theories of the stage to Barrault, who quickly assimilated these ideas into his developing technique. In fact, it is in Barrault's writings that Artaud's concepts take their most lucid form. Barrault's memoirs acknowledge the enormity of Artaud's influence.[10] In the end, it was Artaud who led Barrault away from the rigid aesthetics of Decroux toward a total theater: "The theatre which is no thing, but makes use of everything—gestures, sounds, screams, light, darkness. . . ."[11] This theater of "spiritual signs" was to be a nonrepresentational presentation of transcultural archetypes.[12] Artaud believed the theater could alter cultural consciousness through an assault on the senses and thus used a primitive and direct sensory communication process. "The reality of imagination and dreams will appear there on an equal footing with life."[13] Artaud decried the wordiness of realistic stage language. He believed the goal of the theater should be "to make a metaphysics out of language, gestures, attitudes, sets, and music,"[14] to create a "poetry in space."[15] Following the prescriptions of Artaud, Barrault altered his course.

Barrault says he now is "in quest of the meaning" behind the action, the significance that would put gesture in a different sphere of consciousness, transcending the mere duplication of the spoken word. Mime must be seen as "an act and not a language," as contrasted with nineteenth-century pantomime with its literal meaning.[16] Barrault explains the ramifications of linguistic analogies.

If miming only consists in expressing silent speech, its only value lies in the comical and the effete aspect of the incapacity to express oneself silently. If the details and the expression are excessive, the style of pantomime falls into comic puerility. Yet pantomime is an art which can become as noble and majestic as all the arts. There can be a tragic pantomime. This kind of thing is well known to oriental artists.[17]

Barrault acknowledges a great debt to the philosophy and techniques of oriental theater, and, like Artaud, he is fascinated by its "metaphysical tendencies."[18] On the other hand, although much of Decroux's style resembles that of the Japanese actor, especially the sculptural pose *(mie)* of the Noh, he repudiates the oriental influence, excoriating its emphasis on hand and arm gesture.[19]

Barrault believes that in freeing mime from any relationship to prosaic language, it is possible to give it tragic dimensions. This is in opposition to the comic thrust of the old pantomime.

> Modern mime, striving after purity, seeks to forswear this dumb language. It aims at . . . the expansion of the soul, what in tragedy is called the recitative. What is new in modern mime is its capacity for touching the tragic.[20]

Although Decroux reviled the gratuitous comic effect of the old pantomime, he never fully explored the relationship between mime and tragedy. He dealt more with the pure physical level of gesture than with the metaphysical during the period that he and Barrault worked together.

In dealing with Decroux, the division between nineteenth-century pantomime and the Decroux theories became evident. The difference between Barrault and Decroux is a subtler one and lies more in philosophy than in technique, for Barrault implemented the Decroux *gymnastique* in order to reach his new goals.

Barrault's conviction was that the new mime must possess a dimension beyond both the linear sequence of events of the old pantomime and the new codification of Decroux. Barrault realized that

> In mime there are actually two kinds of *"materiel plastique"*: on the one hand there is the gesture that serves simply to denote action, and on the other there is the gesture comparable to the recitative of a tragedy, the gesture that in and of itself is all things, the gesture that, standing alone, is of poetic substance.[21]

Thus, for Barrault, there is the prosaic gesture that depicts a tangible action, recognizable only as the verb it depicts, and the gesture that can be likened to an image or symbol. In the latter, its evocative quality is the source of its significance, and meaning is determined by the subjective response of the audience. When mime is a series of such gesture-symbols, it becomes "poetry in transformations."[22] It should be noted that this does not necessarily imply an abstraction of movement, for in later examples it shall be demonstrated that this quality is usually imputed to tangible events. Barrault believed a mime "should not have to explain himself, meaning should be evident, and above all one should not be incomprehensible under the guise of being poetic."[23] "Using his imagination, the mime transposes realism and sentiment, inventing a poetic reality. This transposition is not a deformation. Poetry is not caricature."[24] Thus Barrault is less concerned with rebelling against realism than Decroux. He seeks instead an artistic restatement of reality. Writing of Decroux's mime statuaire, Barrault states:

> It is certainly the most interesting of all that attempts to be a truly modern mime, but I take the liberty of saying that it does not satisfy me, for it deforms corporal expression rather than rendering it "truer than truth."
> . . . a good mime should not be a deformed actor. On the contrary, he should be capable of acting in a realistic play as his gestures could conform to the situation by virtue of their simplicity and truth.[25]

Barrault is seeking the poetry of sincerity, a truth rooted in the tenets of psychological realism.

Barrault's distinction between the two levels of gesture (the tangible realistic and the imagistic or symbolic) is based on his understanding that "the man who acts in a certain way has an emotional perception of his conduct that can be different from his actual movements."[26] He explicates further by differentiating between objective and subjective mime: Objective mime is the effect produced through the implementation of the early Decroux technique, with all its advances toward a better understanding of the physical aspects of mime. It is *le contrepoids* and *le raccourci*. It is the illusion of reality. It can be defined as the muscular changes perceivable on the physical countenance of the performer. But Barrault's *mime subjectif* gives *l'attitude* a cosmic dimension. *Mime subjectif* is defined by Barrault as "the study of the states of the soul, as translated into corporeal expression. It is the metaphysical attitude of man in space."[27] Here Artaud's concepts meld with those of Barrault. "As long as mime remains objective, that is as long as it is a propless exercise whose goal is to give the illusion that such and such an object exists, it is obsolete."[28]

To the objective and subjective mime, Barrault adds the level of the imagination. His schema is as follows:

Objective level	What is perceptible to the outsider.
Subjective level	Man's perception of his own actions, often differs from what he actually does.
Imaginary level	Man's imagination transforms what is objective or subjective provoking emotions, i.e., fear, joy, based on his interpretation.[29]

Barrault believes that comprehension of the interaction of these three levels gave oriental and classical Greek theater their tragic depth. He feels that implementation of this concept could add similar dimensions to modern mime, and senses that the old pantomime never confronted this range of expressive possibilities.

> The language of gestures has a side which is both charming and obsolete, belonging to comedy. This is the difference between comedy and tragedy. The new silent mime has a cosmic bearing . . . it is direct, there are no detours . . . death is faced head on. However, in comedy, you can resort to frills and pirouettes. . . . This is not pejorative, but it is a distinction. In the Commedia dell'Arte, for instance, things take place which are not only tragic but atrocious; yet they are always treated with pirouettes and light-hearted spirit.[30]

Thus the new mime deals not with the unidimensional characters of the old pantomime, the stock types capable of surviving all adversity, but portrays instead characters capable of suffering, of pain, of interior anguish. Barrault believes the noblest goal of the new mime is to reach tragic proportions, thereby overcoming the limitations of the comic repertory, which he condemns as the source of pantomime's waning popularity. He therefore expounds the theory of tragic mime:

> What is *le mime tragique?*
> Man thrown into this universe maintains a constant relationship with himself and with the outer world. . . . When the weight of the interior being gains ground on the weight of the exterior world, man acts according to his will. When the

weights balance in the opposite direction, man submits to
whatever the universe imposes on him. . . . Tragedy deals
with man caught in this duel. . . .

As soon as I find myself in possession of this interior world,
I have been sentenced to death . . . my conduct will be a
struggle against death, against time. . . . The body fights to
delay the hour of capitulation and truth.[31]

Up to this point, Barrault is merely stating a view of tragedy
that could be applied easily to any theatrical form. However, his
redefining of the physical mime technique in terms relevant to
tragedy gives a whole new significance to traditional movement
exercises and adds a dimension to corporal expression.

in view of the imminent peril described in Barrault's
definition of the tragic state of man, the body's defenses must
be on a constant alert in order for man to survive in a hostile
world. The body operates as a well-organized system comprised
of the following:

The harvesting inward, or the visceral being.
Potency, or sexual life.
The defenses, or nervous system.
The initiative, or intellectual life.
. . . All of these are subject to the will of the central
committee: the brain.[32]

The way in which these four facets of our inner being organize
themselves in relation to the outer world creates a projected
personality, a demeanor, or what Barrault calls le contenance:

The continual stages of our interior life are called our
countenances.
From the moment the infant lets out its first cry, the new-
born baby has a countenance. . . .
Every human countenance presents a problem for which
we must find the givens.
This is the first tense of mime: the countenance, or man
and his inner self.[33]

Upon closer examination, it becomes clear that Barrault's
countenances are a psychological restatement of Decroux's attitudes: for if attitude is character and style, then countenance,
as the totality of the inner workings of man, must also be
character. The major difference between the two concepts is

that whereas *l'attitude* deals with just the man, *le contenance* deals with man in relation to his individual psyche and to the cosmos. For to Barrault, character and style are only significant in terms of what they reveal of the individual's relationship with the outer world. Each countenance must make us ask: Why is X like that? The mime must know the answer; the public must seek to discover it through its interpretation of the performance. This is the key to Barrault's approach to character.

Through his countenance, man gives off vibrations that interact with the elements around him.

> Man, through his radiation, is enveloped in a magnetic halo. This halo touches exterior objects even before the skin comes in contact with them. The magnetic halo will vary in density according to the vitality or education of the man. The mime must above all else be aware of this boundless contact with the things around him.[34]

Thus the configuration of the four facets of man's physiological self (visceral, sexual, nervous, and intellectual) determine the level of contact he will have with the outer world. The mime must create a character by reaching the same radiation level as the character he is projecting.

The mime must be aware of atmospheric pressure, for the world around him also creates a magnetic field. He must see each movement as pushing through the weight of the air and be so conscious of the physical weight of the hostile world as to engage in a perpetual combat for even the air he breathes. It is only this profound sense of his environment that can enable the mime to give any significance to his actions.

> Thus the outer world contains all that we need for survival, and all from which we must escape. It is up to man to discriminate between the two using the directions-*indications* furnished him by his senses, instincts and body.
> This is the second tense of mime: directions-*indications* or man and the outer world.[35]

According to Barrault, man is caught between what he is in himself *(contenance)* and what he receives from his environment (directions-*indication*). In order to overcome this conflict, "Man must build the bridge of his actions. This will be the third tense of mime."[36]

In summary, man is caught between two opposing forces—his desire to survive and a hostile world that conspires to bring on his death. His countenance is the weapon he uses in this strife according to the directions he receives from his senses. He will put his entire body at his disposition in the struggle for existence, so that his actions will construct the precarious balance with which he must live. The mime must determine the action that will best express the essential conflict of each drama.

Barrault's ties to psychological realism are reflected in his mime theories' relationship to character. In applying his aesthetics to technique, he approaches character through identification with a set of physical needs through which he reconstructs an emotional past, thereby arriving at a justification for the *contenance*. Compared to the techniques of others, Barrault's orientation is existential, assuming that physiological states occur prior to the emotive. What is significant is the emphasis Barrault places on character. This, too, sets him apart from Decroux.

Barrault even uses character to differentiate between mime and dance, thereby giving his analysis of the difference between the two arts. As a result of his concept of *contenance*, timing in mime is the function of character. Timing in dance remains the result of music.

The elements of Decroux's mime grammar find direct parallels in Barrault's system: *Attitude* equals *contenance;* the verb is analagous to the action. However, the scope of Barrault's terminology is different from that of Decroux. To the latter, the verb meant only the movement initiated by the torso, but Barrault's concept of action concerns the way man moves in order to deal with environmental forces, and is a reflection of individual psychology. Once again Barrault extracts an element from Decroux's technique and places it in a dramatic context.

Barrault's explication of the *action* is a restatement of the Decroux *gymnastique,* but linked to his view of tragedy through the theories of Artaud.

All of man's movements can be summed up in two essential ones:
To pull.
To push.
The point of concentration being the center of the stomach: the navel.

Life consists of pulling towards one's self or away from one's self,
And the self: It's the navel.[37]

Thus all movement may be analyzed as being concentric or eccentric in relation to the spinal column. The action indicates whether the individual is dominating his environment, or if instead he is its victim. The push is the aggressive thrust for survival. The pull is the outer world gaining ground on man's will.

In Decroux's earlier technique, all movement was considered to emanate from the spinal column, it is interesting that in this passage Barrault refers to the navel as the focal point. This shift is significant, for it is from the lower abdomen that not only all movement but also all respiration originates. The mechanics of the diaphragm justify finding the source of the breath in this biological area. Hence, placement of the body center in the pelvic region creates a physical focal point enabling a coordination between respiration and action, providing the vital link between *contenance* and action. This provides the basis for implementation of Artaud's theory of the *Kabbale,* his mystic interpretation of the power of the respiratory process related to the occult and magic power of the ancient Hebrew Kabbala.

Barrault uses the *Kabbale* to link his philosophy to technique. Breathing is the basis of life, and as such it is most often an unconscious process. The conscious manipulation of respiratory rhythm is the source of the creation of character. If the actor learns to control the alchemy of respiration, he can put himself in a predetermined physiological or emotional state. The respiratory process must be analyzed so the actor can draw upon it scientifically.

The chest dilates and receives air. It contracts and gives out air. It can also tense and retain air suspending all exchanges. This is the primitive triad of life: to receive, to give, to retain. The triad of respiration is: Inhalation, Exhalation, Retention. . . .
    To receive is the feminine tense.
    To give is the masculine tense.
    To withhold is the neutral tense.
This is the kabbalistic triad.[38]

An analogy can be drawn between this triad and the three primary colors:

yellow	blue	red
neutral	masculine	feminine[39]

As the colors can be combined to form all hues, the masculine, feminine and neutral breath can be combined to form all emotional states, all characters. Tones are modulated by the degree of influx the environment has on the individual, creating shadow and light. Here the theory of the tragic mime ties to the technical respiratory process, for the nature of theatrical expression and character becomes the result of respiration combined with *contenance* and *action*. The more aggressive the character, the more he emphasizes exhalation and the push. The more passive character succumbs to the feminine process. Barrault explains how this can be used as a vital acting technique.

> An example: despite my will, the exterior imposes inhalation. It is therefore a "passive" action. I take in air that is not wanted (as I would an idea that offended me by force). When I can stand it no longer I give out the air that was imposed on me in an active inhalation. Then I close myself.
> But soon after, in fear of asphyxiation, the air comes in again against my will, etc. If I deliver my self up to this rhythm during two or three minutes, I will actually feel in my unconscious respiration the state of anger.[40]

The same theory can be linked to the concept of action:

Pull	Push	Retention
Receive	Give	Retain
Feminine	Masculine	Neutral[41]

Following these analogies, the movement of the spine and torso can also be analyzed according to the kabbalistic triad.

Thus the source of all movement and breath, ergo, character and art is rooted in the configuration of the triad of mystic forces.

The theory of the *Kabbale* leads Barrault to repudiate the

rule of silence in mime. As sound is the result of breath, he believes it is impossible to isolate sound from movement, "for they are both of the same fabric: the result of muscular contraction and respiration."[42] "My question," asks Barrault: "Is there a flaw in mime? Is it sufficient to create the complete character of life? Mime is part of respiration, and one must truly grit the teeth not to make a sound with a breath, and if this sound goes through certain centers of the body, one is so close to the word."[43] Therefore, in opposition to Decroux's vehement early refutation of language and sound, Barrault believes that mime finds its source in silence but need not be silent.

Technical implementation of the *Kabbale* should enable the actor to portray "the magic of life; religion which is physical sensation pushed to an extreme."[44] Barrault learned from Artaud that the theater can be the site of ritual. With the triad of the *Kabbale,* Barrault says "Artaud gave me a key for which I had to find the lock."[45]

The theory of Jean-Louis Barrault is a unique combination of the mysticism of Artaud, the techniques of Decroux, and Dullin's concept of sincerity. More than anything else it represents Barrault himself, who selected and synthesized the ideas of his three mentors, adding to Decroux's *mime statuaire* the dimension of psychological character, philosophically expressed in *le mime subjectif,* and technically realized through a union of Artaud's *Kabbale* and Decroux's *gymnastique.* Although Barrault believes in psychological realism, he does not feel the necessity of an accompanying realistic environment (that is, realistic sets, action or situation) in which this character is to function. Thus Barrault's productions tend to dramatize the inner life of man set against a nonnaturalistic background, often rendered by symbolism or expressionism. This paradox is the natural expression of *le mime tragique,* which is rooted in the conflict between man and his environment. This unique blend of the real and the surreal enable him to make of the stage "a magic space, a world of carnal poetry."[46]

In a letter dated May 1935 (one month prior to the performance of Barrault's first major production), he wrote what can be considered a summary of his mime theory:

This mime, I believe, has not the feeling of pantomime, nor of a school, nor of a fixed aesthetics. It strives to be purely animal: The face becomes a natural mask, the concentration being respiratory.

I don't wish to write a detailed theoretical exposition, for only practical realization of concepts counts. I work as I breathe. . . .[47]

A 1935 dramatic adaptation of the Faulkner novel *As I Lay Dying* became the first vehicle for a theatrical realization of Barrault's theories. "*Tandis que j'agonise* was a subject which permitted me to make my own manifesto; and it was based in silence as all the characters lived in silence."[48]

Barrault changed the title of his production from *Tandis que j'agonise* to *Autour d'une mère*. The novel, about a Southern family, and the events surrounding the mother's death and carrying of the body to her hometown for burial, was a source of great excitement to the young actor. With its diverse subjective narrations of the events by various characters, who distort the story according to their individual emotional structures, the story appeared to be a perfect vehicle for Barrault's new mime technique, which explored the inner man through his movement, gesture, and attitude in space. Thus he was inspired by the novel the create a mime montage. The mise en scène was a unique combination of the technical lessons he had learned from Decroux and his own profound mime philosophy. It was in every way a repudiation of the old pantomime and its imitation of reality. Barrault did not want the new mime to seek gestural expressions for words in the way a mute would use sign language. He implemented his new nonliterate vocabulary of gesture, rendering emotion or thought in imagistic form. This image-movement language did not necessitate a naturalistic time-space continuum. The logical sequence of reality could be sacrificed to obtain greater depth of meaning. Such an approach leaves the deciphering of significance up to the audience, thereby forcing them to take a more active intellectual and emotional role in the performance.

The audience for the opening night was comprised of members of the artistic community who had heard of Barrault's undertaking and turned out to see him make a fool of himself:

Impending catastrophe put all Paris in a state of joy. The curtain went up, exposing a troupe of naked actors with their genitals barely covered. . . .
 A storm of laughter and animal cries followed. Never mind, the play went on. The actors threw daggers at me with

their eyes. We continued. The public calmed down. The silence. . . . I had won.[49]

The scene that assuaged the skeptical audience's doubts as to
the viability of the new concept in mime was the training of the
wild horse. Here Barrault transformed himself into "a marvelous sort of centaur."[50] The horse was represented by a painted
wooden head fastened to Barrault's belt. With the lower half of
his body, Barrault played the prancing, butting, kicking animal,
struggling to rid itself of its rider; with the upper half he was
Jewel, the man, beating the wild beast into submission. Eventually the horse submitted and started to prance in a regular
rhythm, followed by a gradual acceleration into a gallop that
carried the "centaur" off the stage. At any moment in this sequence, Barrault's body would have been an expressive unit
communicating a comprehensible idea, a manifestation of *l'attitude*. The simultaneous rendering of man and animal with two
separate indentities (as opposed to the mythological unified
centaur) was an innovation of the new mime that changed the
logical relationships of reality into nonnaturalistic imagistic
ones. Here we see "the expression of the body directly serving
an action. Plastic exaltation pushed as far as gesture symbol."[51]

The preperformance forecasts of impending disaster were so
overwhelming that the cast mutinied. Out of fear of failure, the
actress who was to play the mother refused to go on opening
night. Instead of canceling the performance, Barrault decided
to play the part himself, differentiating between this and his
own role through a weird costume for the mother, comprised
of a grillwork mask with steel buttons for the eyes, a wig of long
black hair, and a long multicolored skirt. By transposing three
scenes, Barrault was able to play both parts. The mother had
up to then

> been just like all the other characters, just as human, no more
> human; but, by the addition of the mask and this rig-out—
> naked male torso over a wide skirt, black mane of hair like
> those shrunken Mexican heads stuffed with sand, the charac-
> ter of the mother became a kind of idol-like totem, and raised
> the theme of the drama up to the level of tragedy.[52]

The mother's death was created through a pattern of respiration. Barrault describes this scene as follows:

The mother went through a slow painful agony which I translated right up to the moment of death by a series of long calculated breathings that made a ghastly effect, corresponding with the scrapings of the saw of the carpenter-son, who, at is mother's instructions, was, during her agony, making her coffin.[53]

It was the portrayal of a duel between a woman struggling for her life and an inexorable external death force. This is an example of the conflict that Barrault feels enables modern mime to reach tragic dimensions. During her battle with death, the neighbors move slowly around her chanting: "La voisine n'est pas bien, la voisine va périr, va-pér-ri-ir." The tempo of their chant is steadily increased. This establishes a driving rhythm representing the onslaught of death and gives the dying woman another external obstacle to overcome in her fight for life. The conflict between inner will and external forces is thus heightened. The repetitive chant is a realization of Artaud's directive "to consider language as the form of incantation."[54]

The moment of the mother's death has been long hailed as Barrault's theatrical coup. He created a vertical death.

The chant and the sawing stop on an inhalation. The mother's hand, which had been raised to the head in the movement made when one is gazing into the distance, descends slowly in silence; as water drains, life is emptied out. Behind the movement of the hand which extends along the entire body, a cadaver-like rigidity occurs. She is dead.[55]

The weird sound of the saw made by the son while sawing his mother's coffin illustrates the attempt to find an organic link between sound and gesture. In this case, the technique gives life to an inanimate object—the saw, while creating a counterpoint to the human heavings of the dying mother. From this point on, the coffin the son made is represented "in two ways: by a symbolic coffin-shaped plank about ten inches long and in a purely imaginary manner by gestures of the actors as they pretend to heave something on their shoulders."[56] After her death, the mother is resurrected as a young woman, a reversal of the realistic sequence of events.

While her mother is dying, the young girl of the family, Dewey Dell, makes love with her boyfriend in the cotton field.

After her lover goes, she rises, takes a deep breath, and then relaxes into a state of animal happiness. She feels twice around the fullness of her breasts; her hands descend to her stomach, then to her buttocks, undulating her dress. In a surge of femininity, she fixes her hair and her clothes. She stops suddenly. Surprised, she stares at her navel. Her body gets heavier as she slowly takes on the walk of a pregnant woman. This scene also is based on a sequence of autonomous *attitudes* or *contenances,* each communicating a total idea. The events depicted are shown at an accelerated speed, going from conception to advanced pregnancy in moments. The philosophy of the old pantomime was such that it would have been unlikely to find conception and pregnancy revealed through a continuous process. The audience would not have seen a character growing pregnant but rather the act of lovemaking followed by the state of being pregnant.

The river, overflowing its banks, must be crossed to bring the mother's body to the family burial ground. The turbulent water is mimed by actors "who dance from the footlights to downstage [*sic*], their arms extended and undulating to express waves."[57] The crossing of the river becomes a battle between the characters trying to survive against the current and the actors who mime the violent flooded river. Their bodies interlock in the strife between man and the elements. It is a scene that occurs on two levels simultaneously. The characters, defining their objects and objectives, play the realistic drama of a dangerous river crossing, while the river with which they struggle is mimed in a nonnaturalistic fantasy fashion by other actors who transform themselves into waves of water. At one point, one of the river-actors drowns the wooden head used to represent the horse; thus the drowning is an interrelationship of images and symbols. The sound of the fast-flowing water is made by the actors to give another dimension to the life of the river. This works the same way the sawing noise did earlier. It also provides a contrast to the sounds of the characters gasping for air while caught in the deluge, thereby emphasizing man's struggle against external forces, and conforming to Barrault's definition of "*le mime tragique.*"

In the last scene of the play, Barrault captures the movement of a city. In the background a record of city sounds is played, while on the stage there are two actors playing pedestrians and two playing automobiles, while a policeman directs their traffic.

The drivers argue and blow their horns, moving rapidly to create a great hub of activity representative of the urban environment. Thus the set is changed through gesture and rhythm, requiring no use of realistic stage design.

Of course, in many places Barrault called upon the techniques he had developed with Decroux for certain effects; e.g., the idea of walking in places to create the illusion of traveling long distances. Identification with the elements, a basic technique, was implemented; however, its application was a most theatrical one, as evidenced by the creation of the river. In the scene where one of the characters sets fire to a barn containing the remains of his mother, he eventually becomes the fire by capturing its respiration and movement. It is not the transformation of a man into an element that is innovative, but rather the use of the *Kabbale* to effect this identification, which becomes a means of communicating the character's emotional involvement with the act he committed. This links the theory of *le mime tragique* with the *Kabbale,* necessitating the viewing of the mime as a physically and psychologically integrated being, quite different from the stock character of the old pantomime.

The key concept in this mise en scène is therefore the painting of a subjective tableau with gesture, exemplifying the intrinsic link between body and idea. This goal gave gesture a symbolic aura. Artaud had this to say:

> His gestures are so beautiful that they seem to take on a symbolic meaning. Yet there are certainly no symbols in this production of Jean-Louis Barrault, and if there is one reproach one can make with relation to his movements, it is that they give the illusion of a symbol while defining - reality. . . .[58]

It is here that Barrault differs from Artaud's strict belief in metaphysics and symbolism, and finds himself closer to Dullin. For while Artaud says "that the drama was born in the sky,"[59] Barrault claims that "the art of theatre consists of the recreation of life observed from the angle of Silence, of the Present, through the means available to the human being."[60] Although Barrault appears to be influenced by realism, it remains that Artaud sensed *Autour d'une mère* to be a moment of stage magic; that he believed the nonnaturalistic base for the mise en scène opened new vistas of theatrical possibilities, for in this produc-

tion one could discover "new relationships between sound, gesture, and voice."[61] When the opening-night performance
ended, Barrault found an ecstatic Artaud at the stage door. The
two friends galloped off into the night emulating Barrault's
magic centaur.

*Autour d'une mère,*as the first major production to incarnate
the new mime, became "not only a precise reference point in
Barrault's artistic biography, but also one in the history of
French theater. It is an event to which one can refer for a better
understanding of an artistic moment in time."[62] After seeing
the production, Jouvet summed up its importance:

> Here I see the distance which separates two generations. All
> that we formulated in our heads during the era of the Vieux
> Colombier, you have circulating in your blood. Digestion has
> taken place.[63]

As a postscript it should be noted that not only was *Autour
d'une mère* a point of change in French theater, but it exists as a
clear demarcation line in the career of Jean-Louis Barrault, for
it was this mise en scène that established him in the Parisian
theatrical circle. He felt ready to set out on his own without the
guidance of the men who had formed him. He wrote to Dullin
to inform him that he would not return to the Atelier:

> I was carried for three years in the belly of the Atelier. In
> June I was born. The work that I performed that month cut
> the umbilical cord. I was born. And I screamed. And I
> screamed.[64]

Autour d'une mère also marked the final separation between
Barrault and Decroux. The performance made it all too clear
that they were headed in different directions. Barrault, with his
free-flowing style was the seducer of audiences. Decroux, with
his rigid aesthetics, alienated the public. Whereas Barrault desired a total theater of sound and movement, Decroux was
fanatically devoted to pure mime. Barrault recounts:

> When I created *Autour d'une mère,* he [Decroux] found that
> I was in error . . . and in a way, he was right: For I was
> naturally interested in theatre, and in the theatre there is
> *expression corporelle;* but it wasn't in my nature to specialize
> exclusively in mime.[65]

Autour d'une mère was the first stage of what was to become Barrault's unique brand of total theater, for it meant, first and foremost, total use of the human being as an expressive organism, seeing "the human body as the essential instrument of theatre."[66] Barrault maintains this view, although his work is constantly shifting emphasis. But these changes are a natural artistic phenomenon to a man like Barrault who believes "the theatre to be in permanent evolution."[67]

Barrault believes that the production of *Autour d'une mère* marks another turning point in his life: a movement away from the individual toward the social, and a politicization of his art. The Atelier dealt with man and saw the theater as the art of man as an individual. The period of the troupe of the Grenier des Grands-Augustins (1936–1939) began the era of socially relevant theater in the career of Jean-Louis Barrault.

In the spring of 1937, after Barrault had managed to save some money from his performances in two films, *Sous les yeux d'Occident* and *Hélène,* he invested it all in a new production— *Numance (The Siege of Numantia)* by Cervantes. The play is a romantic retelling of the barbaric conquest of Numantia by the Romans, who had so starved the citizens during a fifteen-month siege, that upon taking possession of the city, they found only one child alive. The others killed each other off to avoid suffering, and the last surviving child chose to commit suicide, marking the Roman conquest in futile tragedy. The play, which is "a series of disjointed incidents linked together by the almost oracular discourses of allegorical figures,"[68] becomes for Jean-Louis Barrault "the basis for an exploration of the theatrical medium."[69]

Considering Barrault's shift toward political relevance, the play was a logical choice of subject matter, coming during the Spanish Civil War and at a time when Europe was besieged by the military dictatorships of Hitler and Mussolini. Barrault's mise en scène underlined the contemporary references:

One sees an army of legionnaires coming forth, automatons marching with jerkings of their stiffened legs. Their leader walks ahead, moving his arms as if they were sticks, punctuating these maneuvers by a bizarre German onomatopoeia.[70]

Even when they are asleep, their deepened breaths sound as if they were executed to precise order.[71]

This choreography of the army was an all too vivid and recognizable image!

The reviewers of the Communist press in France were quick to point out the relationship between the play and the fascist menace: "How can one help but think of the war in Spain against Italian and German invaders when confronted with the inhuman suffering inflicted on the people of Numantia,"[72] wrote the critic for *Humanité.* From *Le Peuple:* "One cannot escape thinking of the present day Spanish tragedy when confronted by this play."[73]

Barrault saw *Numance* as the perfect vehicle for a synthesis of his mime theory and elements of total theater incorporating his new social conscience:

> On the social schema, I contributed to the cause of the Spanish Republicans—the individual was respected, liberty was glorified. On the metaphysical level of the theatre, I penetrated the realm of the chimerical—death, blood, famine, furor and rage. Dance, mime, song, reality, surreality. The river, the fire, the magic. My total theatre. I lost myself in it. *Numance:* the verification that allowed me to go further.[74]

The plight of the Numantians met all the prerequisites of *le mime tragique.* The situation is a vivid portrayal of the struggle of the inner man infringed upon by outer forces. Caught in the duel, he chooses hunger and death as the nobler fate. His *contenance* marks the decision, while his actions must bridge the unfortunate gap between what he is, in and of himself, and what is being imposed upon him. The inevitability of death is all-consuming, there is no escape, no comic trapdoor. Certainly there is no more poignant description of man's tragic plight than realization of the theme, "Viva la Muerte."

The play is constructed as a series of poetic episodes that Barrault transforms into visual tableaux. Through mime, he is able to express events impossible to depict in any naturalistic style; e.g. cannibalism and the mass massacre of the Numantian women by their own men so as not to leave them as whores for the Romans. Allegorical figures appear as masked phantoms: War, Hunger, and Pestilence unify the epic action. Using elements of the Suzanne Bing technique that he had learned from Decroux, Barrault choreographs "a ballet of masks."[75] This is not mime in silence. The action is interspersed with portions of text, and loudspeakers emit appropriate sound effects and music.

Barrault sees *Numance* as a demonstration of

the virtue of gesture, the resources of the body, the plasticity of the verb, the importance of consonants, the danger of over-dependence on vowel sounds, the prosody of spoken language, the use of long and short syllables, the iamb and the anapest, the art of respiration.[76]

Barrault's total theater uses all the expressive channels available: moving sets, lights, sound effects, music, film, etc. But it depends most upon use of the actor's entire being as an integrated tool. Although Barrault was a confrère of Brecht and Piscator, he relied less on mechanical devices and much more than they on muscular plasticity, on the new mime as an element of the production. In this respect he was closer in feeling to Meyerhold. Referring to the latter, Barrault says,

I would have had a weakness for this man had I known him. This sentence of his gave me much to think about—"It is only through the domain of athletics that one can approach the domain of the theatre."[77]

Certainly this physical bias was the dominant force in his mise en scène. He claimed, "We want to give expressive force back to drama, so that it can become a scenic sculpture of our sentiments, a living model."[78]

The new mime was still too novel to be universally accepted as a valid means of theatrical expression. The conservative critics railed at this emphasis on corporal expression:

This theatrical art that is so close to his heart, and of which he has formed such a high ideal, he is willing to subjugate to the methods and ideals of a gymnastics teacher. . . .

He [Barrault] will excuse me for not believing in the renewal of the theatre through a regimen of *"interpretation corporelle,"* for when a good quarter of an hour goes by between the curtain going up and the first time an actor utters a word, I cannot avoid a certain impatience no matter how successful the ballet before me.[79]

The violent reaction to the physical partiality of this mise en scène seems incomprehensible today, with our theater's life-blood coming from such groups as The Open Theatre, The Manhattan Project, and The Polish Laboratory Theatre. But Barrault reminds us that the spectacle of half-naked actors displaying primal emotions was a shock to the audience of the 1930s.[80] Despite the critical lack of compassion for his efforts, Barrault continued working in the same direction, determined to gain respect for his new mime.

Barrault went on to adapt yet another novel, *La Faim* by Jules Laforgue, into what he called an *action dramatique*. He justified his choice of material claiming, "I did not want to adapt the novel, I wanted to perform a theatrical 'realization,'"[81] for "in the theatre, a symbolic object or the attitude of the actor multiplies and suggests several continuations, whereas the novel outlines only one reality."[82] There were, of course, those who were neither in agreement with his choice nor swayed by his defense. From Antoine we read, "To tell the truth, it's really more of a parody of a masterpiece evoking a weary boredom."[83] From Brisson,

> What this is really about is the need to throw himself into a play, and not a semi-novel or one-quarter ballet, to think the play out, to draw it out of its text, and put it on stage so we can see it live its natural life. . . .[84]

From yet another critic,

> If instead of giving himself to futile exercises of transposition he would only put his talents to the service of a work written directly for the theatre, I maintain that the text, the dialogue, would furnish the essential element. . . .[85]

Barrault did have his supporters. From Benjamin Crémieux,

> Considering the lack of contemporary masterpieces, one must return to works of the past. This is what M. Barrault did in resuscitating *Numance* by Cervantes, and it is what he must continue to do, while awaiting the author of his dreams.[86]

Artaud provides a vehement justification of Barrault's position,

> Instead of continuing to rely upon texts considered definitive and sacred, it is essential to put an end to the subjugation of the theatre to the text, and to recover the notion of a kind of unique language halfway between gesture and thought.[87]

With his emphasis on the physical technique of the actor, Barrault feels no obligation to limit his repertory to the traditional material of the theater. He chooses, instead works that enable him to communicate sensation directly, works that reveal "the silent comportment of primitive beings."[88] His next undertaking, *La Faim*, was just such a work.

La Faim deals with the hardships of a young writer, Tanguen, in his battle against death by hunger. As he is more and more consumed by his need for food, the world around him assumes a distorted perspective. The mise en scène enables us to see life through the eyes of the starving young man, in a series of subjective tableaux. The psychological focus of the work is expressionist in nature.

As the words of the novel are spoken by a narrator, the actors create the physical reality of the text. The action traces events in Tanguen's struggle for life. He is seen searching for money and work in a hostile world that takes no heed of him. While Tanguen summons the strength to continue, barely able to walk, crowds pass him on the street carrying out the mechanical movements of their daily life. Under Barrault's direction, they become a "ballet of automatons,"[89] an example of "gesture symbol." This passage is an implementation of the duel between the inner man and the exterior world intrinsic to the theory of the tragic mime as discussed earlier.

Tanguen climbs the six flights to his garret room in a sequence of mimed ascent. The slides projected as a backdrop show different perspectives of the stairway, heightening the illusion of the climb. Here Barrault has combined the Decroux technique (simulation of walking up stairs) with an element of Piscatorian stage technology to achieve a unique effect.

Once in his room, Tanguen is so weakened by hunger that he begins to hallucinate. The junk furniture around him begins to dance, encircling him, while the phantoms of his subconscious are personified in nightmarish vividness. Pursued by his hallucinations, he tried to flee them in a mad chase scene. The play becomes the drama of a man "who, feeling his rational powers escaping him, tries desperately to keep a grip on his sanity despite unconquerable physical and moral torture."[90] Barrault saw this physical realization of the struggle for survival as the personification of *le mime tragique*. This scene is also a manifestation of both objective and subjective mime operating simultaneously, for here the clearly observable reality is pitted against man's perception of his self in terms of an inner reality. Of *La Faim*, Barrault writes:

> In this production I experimented with many new concepts:
> The play between the actor and lighting (climbing the stairs),
> simultaneous scenes, scenes of incoherence, words which
> have no sense, but whose resonance produces a plastic sense
> of conversation and situation. Spoken text with chanted re-
> sponse. Heartbeats and humming, musical effects. And
> above all, man and his double.[91]

La Faim and *Numance* are close to the tenets of Artaud's theater of cruelty, "furnishing the spectator with the truthful pre-
cipitates of dreams, in which his taste for crime, his erotic obses-
sions, his savagery, his chimeras, his utopian sense of life and
matter, even his cannibalism pour out."[92] Once more, Barrault's
close personal relationship with Artaud had its effect on his
artistic development. Underscoring this, he wrote in his latest
book, "I was to adhere with all my being to the definition of an
actor given by Artaud—'The actor: An emotional athlete.' "[93]

The production of *La Faim* triggered much furor among the
critics, both in terms of subject matter and treatment. The reac-
tions were so violent in defense of or against his new mime
theater, that there seemed to be an actual choosing of sides
between the staunch realists and the advocates of total theater.
The single most impressive factor in reading the reviews of this
performance is that no matter what any individual critic had to
say about the style and content, even those of the opposition,
each and every one of them, somewhere in his review, noted
that Jean-Louis Barrault was the most exciting and impressive
talent in the theater of the time. Often this was noted with the
suggestion that he devote his staggering talent to more naturalistic pursuits. To get Frenchmen of various persuasions to
agree unanimously on anything is a great testament to its verac-
ity.

Despite the mass appreciation for Barrault's talents, the criticism was most vigorous. Antoine called the production "painful
because of its visible preoccupation with shocking the audience."[94] The conservative Brisson reacted;

> The general spirit of the work is circa 1925. Vakhtangov and
> Piscator tendencies, surface surrealism, carnival atmosphere
> . . . stylized breathing of crowds projected over megaphones,
> rhythmic movements of actors . . . marriage of the boudoir
> with the factory. . . . Around 1925, these dismemberments
> had their significance, even their interest . . . but today this
> period has been shelved, we know what it was worth. . . .[95]

Another critic echoed the sentiments of Brisson,

> After the war, it was probably necessary to make a brutal rupture with a theatre that was photographic, phonographic, and downright bourgeois that the realists had left to us, and to return to the stage its rights to poetry, carnival, tragedy, and imagination. It was obviously not useless to replace the servile imitation of reality by stylization: Stylization of decors, costumes, and gestures, seeking expressionism out of disgust with naturalism . . . but these were only temporary means and excesses in order to liberate the theatre. . . .

Since then the theatre has rediscovered its rights.[96] But critic Lucien Descaves had this to say, "How far we have come since Le Théâtre Libre and Le Théâtre de l'Oeuvre. . . . We will have taken part in a revolution of theatrical technique realized by an impassioned young actor."[97] Still another critic commented,

> Belated surrealism, anachronistic expressionism, obsolete Piscatorism, post-war technique, exploration of the impasse of tragedy-ballet, rhythmic art with literary pretension, the dancer-actor, and the mime with a voice.
> M. Jean-Louis Barrault, does he really merit these reproaches? . . . as for me, I was totally enrapt by the hallucination.[98]

Undaunted by his critics, Barrault continued in his innovative style. His 1942 production of Paul Claudel's *Le Soulier de Satin* was performed at the Comédie Française, where Barrault's use of "Total Theatre"—special effects and pantomimed shipwrecks—rocked that theatre's conservative audience. His success set a precedent for future endeavors. Barrault implemented similar techniques in his mise en scènes for André Gide's adaptation of Kafka's *The Trial* in 1947, Albert Camus's *L'Etat de Siège* in 1948, and Claudel's *Christophe Colomb* in 1953. More recently, Barrault inserted long lyrical mime passages in his 1968 production—*Rabelais*. In retrospect, it appears that Barrault was ahead of his time. He did in fact synthesize the post–World War I trends, but he added to them the bias of the new mime technique, altering their emphasis.

Barrault attempted to work at his craft during the trying period of the war. In 1943 he starred in *Children of Paradise (Les Enfants du Paradis)*, a cinematic masterpiece that reawakened popular interest in pantomime, and justifiably so, according to

Barrault. "Why has pantomime always been a popular art," he queries, and replies, "for throughout time, the masses have been deprived of their say."[99] The film (which also featured Decroux), is a fiction based on the life of pantomimist Jean-Gaspard Deburau. Upon superficial examination, it appears to be a throwback to the old pantomime. In keeping with the original Deburau style, many of the mime techniques used for this film are reminiscent of *la pantomime blanche;* however, the mime numbers vary in tone from broad Commedia-style comedy to poignant drama. Baptiste, the Deburau character played by Barrault, is a white-faced Pierrot, typical of nineteenth-century pantomime. But Barrault felt he had contemporary relevance, for "Baptiste is a primitive, a child. . . . Naughty at his strongest moments, he can only fight and kill in a dream. When he wakes up, he is content to offer a bouquet to a statue. And the statue accepts."[100] After *Children of Paradise,* Barrault asked Jacques Prévert, the creator of the new Baptiste, to continue supplying him with sketches for the character. But, Barrault lamented,

> My calls have remained unanswered. What a pity, for so many important things could have been expressed through Baptiste, who is surely related to Kafka and to Hamlet. What a splendid satire of our age could take place through him. . . . One need not confine oneself to the old pantomime. . . . Baptiste was something special.[101]

Through Baptiste the audience feels "nostalgia for their lost liberty. One can ask no more of the theatre."[102] Barrault believed that if Baptiste could in any way elucidate modern man's dilemma he was a valid vehicle of expression for the new mime. Barrault felt Baptiste to be a modern personality akin to the Charlie Chaplin character in nature, for

> only Charlie Chaplin knew how to find purity, using the old pantomime as a point of departure. Taking our inspiration from his example, we will perhaps find a new style of silent pantomime for the theatre. But the true problem of modern mime still remains as the elevation of gesture to tragic heights.[103]

With the creation of the Companie Renaud-Barrault in 1946, Barrault seemed to choose a divergent path in the threater. His

marriage to Madeleine Renaud, a French actress of the classical school, was a union of careers, as well as one of love. The artistic end product "resembled neither Jean-Louis nor Madeleine . . . it was a mixture of the two of them, creating a very real new individuality."[104]
Barrault explains:

> After the "fauvisme" of the Atelier, after the emancipation of surrealism, I was ready to receive the classic imprint of the French.
> For many of my friends I was a traitor . . . a coward lacking in character.
> First off, they forgot Madeleine. Love is still love. After the intolerable separation of the war, we were going to live together and be One. . . . We were going to act together, sharing the same cares, the same trials, the same hopes, the same destiny.[105]

Although from time to time Barrault would revive Baptiste, or do a mime number such as *La Fontaine de Jouvence,* or insert a mime passage in a mise en scène, he never again pursued the art of gesture with the vigor he had shown in his youth. He rationalizes his record, saying:

> Out of fifty-four works given in ten years I have produced only three pantomimes; *Baptiste* in 1946, *La Fontaine de Jouvence* in 1947, and *Suites d'une Course* in 1956. Why so few pantomimes? First because it is difficult to find good subjects, and second, because pantomime is still an ill-defined genre. . . . A Pantomime which lasts half an hour requires the same amount of material as a five act play.[106]

Yet throughout his writings there remains the same unfulfilled promise: "For my part, I hope to have the courage to pursue my old dream of continuing work on the blossoming of a tragic mime built on symbols."[107] Although he did not realize his old dream, as late as 1968, echoing Decroux, he wrote the following on the mask:

> The concentration it offers to discover the expressive means of the body is unique . . . the human face is endowed with one hundred little muscles that can change everything in the total expression, and it is delightful for an actor to

erase all this by a mask, and find out what he can do only with his body. The exploration of all possible means of expression within the human being is the essence of total theatre. Most probably we should go to a naked theatre.[108]

In a recent interview Barrault stated: "Having completed my career and my research, I have ended by loving mime more now than ever before."[109]

Why then did he stop developing the new mime? Was it due to his disappointment in the artistic merit of the young Decroux-Barrault disciples?

The young people who have done mime can no longer make the smallest gesture without adding frills and useless movements, giving a false architecture to their actions. The result is a visual mannerism, which upon translation into spoken language would be unbearable.[110]

This dismay may be a plausible explanation for his lack of recent activity in the field, for in a 1972 interview Barrault says,

Contortions on the pretext of performing mime, and mannerism. It is this that stopped me from continuing. But it is because of love of mime that I stopped, and not at all due to indifference.[111]

Barrault had, at a much earlier time, voiced an abhorrence for artificial gesture:

. . . I think a good mime should not be the caricature of an actor, but on the contrary, he should be more capable than all others to act in a realistic drama, as he will know how to use simple and true gesture.[112]

Perhaps his lack of avid travail for the art he admittedly loves so much is based on a profound philosophic observation:

After the marvelous mask exercises executed by Suzanne Bing at the Vieux Colombier, after the often inspiring research by Etienne Decroux, after our all-too-intermittent experiments, after the constant and effective efforts of Marcel Marceau and a few other liberated disciples, I have the impression that mime has once again come to an impasse.[113]

Unfortunately, to date at least, it seems to me that modern

mime offers only a limited range. Either it forks off to the abstract and the obscure when it is explored in depth as by Etienne Decroux in his courageous and exemplary research ... or else it returns to the burlesque, to the old pantomime, as younger mimes are performing it today.[114]

Does this impasse really exist? Is the scope of modern mime indeed limited? An examination of the work of Jacques Lecoq and Marcel Marceau will furnish the answers.

With Decroux caught in the rut of academics, and Barrault abandoning the terrain, the inevitable question seems to be looming before us—Does the new mime have anywhere else to go and anyone to take it there? It is quite possible that it was just in the Barrault personality (loving experiment and risk) to move on to new things. It is a query to remain unanswered until the work of the two still-active advocates of the cause is examined.

For the purposes of this book, we will leave the career of Jean-Louis Barrault in 1946, for although he has since given mime performances, his most significant achievements in the field of mime occured prior to this point. It is imperative, however, to emphasize the phenomenal contribution Barrault has made to the rejuvenation of French theater through the use of mimetic technique. It is, in fact, Barrault who completes the task Jacques Copeau once aspired to. Barrault says Copeau "taught us everything."[115] And Copeau saw in Barrault the epitome of his ideal actor—saying: "Jean-Louis Barrault is from the same school and is inspired by the same principles, but he pushes their consequences further because his technique is more perfect. He respects the text . . . but never misses an opportunity to develop an action or to add an episode of invention."[116] Through his creative imagination and unique talent, Barrault resuscitated the classics and gave new scope to contemporary drama. He expanded the boundaries of realism, and waged war against the vestiges of classical declamation, making the total actor in a total theater acceptable on the French stage. He exalted plastic expression to new heights. "Watching him, one has the feeling that total theatre is not totality of means, but the totality of meaning that can be searched for and discovered in man himself."[117]

Etienne Decroux: *Sport.* **Photo credit: Etienne-Bertrand Weill.**

Etienne Decroux and Maximilien Decroux: *Combat Antique.* **Photo credit: Etienne-Bertrand Weill.**

Etienne Decroux: *Usine.* **Photo credit: Etienne-Bertrand Weill.**

Etienne Decroux: *Meditation.* **Photo credit: Etienne-Bertrand Weill.**

Jean-Louis Barrault: *La Mort.* **Photo credit: Etienne-Bertrand Weill.**

Jean-Louis Barrault: *Le Sonneur de cloches.* **Photo credit: Etienne-Bertrand Weill.**

Jean-Louis Barrault in New York: *Rabelais.* **Photo courtesy of Cultural Services of the French Embassy.**

Marcel Marceau: *Le Manteau.* **Photo courtesy of Cultural Services of the French Embassy.**

Marcel Marceau in New York: *The Tightrope.* **Photo credit: Jim Moore.**

Marcel Marceau: *Bip.* **Photo credit: Etienne-Bertrand Weill.**

Former Lecoq student—Carlo Mazzone Clementi: *Brighella.* **Commedia dell'arte mask by Stanley Allan Sherman, New York. Photo credit: Jim Moore.**

Carlo Mazzone Clementi: *Comedic Clown.* **Photo credit: Jim Moore.**

Mummenschanz. Photo credit: Christian Altorfer. Photo courtesy of ICM Artists.

Mummenschanz. Photo credit: Christian Altorfer. Photo courtesy of ICM Artists.

5

MARCEL MARCEAU
(1923–   )

Twelve years after the great mime collaboration of Barrault and Decroux, Marcel Marceau, a young would-be actor from Strasbourg, came to Paris and to Dullin's Atelier to learn his craft. There he met Decroux, who was still in search of disciples. Decroux, so quick to recognize the unique talents of Barrault, readily perceived Marceau's natural gifts and wasted no time in recruiting him for the new mime. The Atelier again became the site of arduous travail for the cause. But early on the divergence between student and master was apparent:

> It was the winter of 1944–45, harsh, inclement and without heat. Marceau, at that time, was known only as the most brilliant of Decroux's students. The spectacle of these two men solemnly at work, dripping with sweat in that frigid air, had something admirably crazy about it which spiced their work. The teacher was serious to the point of being comic; he demonstrated an impeccable technique, but was strained in the search for the original and the creative. But the budding mime burst forth with originality, with facility, spirit and charm which are the signs of the artist.[1]

These differences were to become more pronounced as time went on.

Marceau, like Barrault, was subject to other influences that were to affect his personal style:

> With Decroux he [Marceau] concentrated on the techniques of *"Mime Statuesque"* [sic], the representation of human at-

titudes and *mime objectif,* making objects visible through the balance of the body. From Dullin's exercises in sincerity, Marceau learned of the importance of emotional authenticity in the contact between artist and spectator.[2]

Marceau's early experiences with Decroux moved him to alter his plans to become a dramatic actor. Shortly after his arrival at the Atelier, he decided to specialize in mime and thus worked diligently to master the Decroux *grammaire,* which was to serve as the basis for all his future work.

Despite his devotion to the Decroux method and to the new mime, Marceau shared Barrault's desire to reach the public more directly, and this naturally prevented a prolonged collaboration with Decroux. As Decroux scorned his public, so Marceau was to court them. Therefore Marceau did what he was obliged to do, and went to meet his audience.[3]

In 1946, Marceau left Decroux to work with Jean-Louis Barrault in *Baptiste* and *Arlequin.*[4] These roles were in the style Barrault so adeptly demonstrated in the film *Children of Paradise (Les Enfants du Paradis):* that is, they were reminiscent of the nineteenth-century lyric Pierrots, but included some character development. They combined the techniques of the ancient mime tradition with Decroux's grammar and concepts of psychological realism. Considering Barrault's stature in the Parisian theater, this collaboration was the next logical step in Marceau's development. It should be noted that in 1946, Barrault was already being pulled away from mime through his collaboration with Madeleine Renaud, and therefore gave mime only a minor role in his repertory. The young Marceau had just discovered his unusual talents in this field, and needed to showcase his newfound prowess. The Companie Renaud-Barrault was clearly not the most attractive cadre for his abilities with its theatrical orientation and the dominance of Barrault, under whose shadow he would be forced to perform. It was thus inevitable that Marceau would soon end his union with Barrault and set out on his own.

In summary, "Marceau, who was the student of Decroux, and in 1946, the partner of Barrault in *Baptiste,* does not discover the true Marcel Marceau until 1947: six years later he is saluted as the resurrector of his art."[5] His relationships with Decroux and Barrault served as the prelude to the career that was to follow.

During the period that Marceau studied with Decroux, there was an emphasis on illusionary mime, which Decroux was later to abandon. References to Decroux's technique in this chapter refer to this early period in Decroux's development. All comparisons of the two men refer to Decroux's technique as it existed in the 1940s. Marceau's work is an expansion of these original explorations. In the past forty years, however, Decroux has moved in different directions. Today, Marceau and Decroux reflect divergent mime styles.

Armed with the Decroux grammar, Marceau attempted to develop a personal mime style. He began performing independently in 1947, the year in which he created the character Bip, whose many adventures have been part of the Marceau repertoire ever since. His first shows consisted of multi-charactered *mimodrames* (silent mime-dramas), which he performed until 1956, at which time Marceau decided to devote himself to solo performances. Since then, his program has been divided between *pantomimes de style,* brief exercises in corporal virtuosity, and Bip numbers. He rigidly maintains Decroux's rule of silence, but uses musical accompaniment for effect. He wears the whiteface of nineteenth-century pantomime. The audience sees a series of movement cameos, each preceded by the stylized display of a title card by an assistant who strikes a sculptural pose. The titles situate the imminent action in the proper context and function like those of the silent Deburau pantomimes.

Although Marceau has done television and film work, most of his presentations have been live performances rendered in the above format. These have brought him worldwide fame. Before examining these performances, it is important to analyze the theories and techniques that have wrought this success.

Decroux and Barrault developed detailed philosophical bases for their techniques, setting the precedent that the modern mime be a theoretician as well as a performer. Jacques Lecoq, the subject of the next chapter, follows in this cerebral tradition. Marceau, on the other hand, seems ill at ease in the role of theorist. He differs from the others in that he is primarily a performer. His intellectual analysis comes after the fact of his accomplishments. Although he makes attempts at philosophizing, he is clearly in his most natural element on stage.

Marceau is a devout believer in the original premise behind

the Decroux *grammaire,* feeling that only through codification could mime become an established art and guarantee its own survival. He writes, "If the Music Hall and circus are dying, it is only because their artists wanted to die with their secrets, and therefore refused to transmit them. . . ."[6] "Classical dance has a style because there is a grammar, and the same thing holds for mime. It is only in this manner that mime can become an art."[7] It is clear that Marceau supports the cerebral aesthetics and rigid structure that Decroux contributed to twentieth-century mime.

Marceau makes restatements of the early Decroux technique that reflect his personal style:

> Mime is the art of the *contrepoids.* In identifying with the object, the mime becomes the object, taking on not only its form, but also its weight. His active means is to express himself through pushing and pulling. . . . Such is the language which can translate the abstract by the concrete, which yields realism through stylization.[8]

This definition of mime reflects Marceau's emphasis on the illusionary style. Interestingly, this passage reveals an unconventional use of the word *realism,* which would be better replaced by *reality.* For in fact, Marceau's stylized technique is antithetical to the demands of realism.

Marceau further defines realistic art in an unusual manner:

> The art of mime should be abstract. This aesthetic representation by the body should be concrete, its architecture must be readable, and its lyric import should be social. Let us not confuse stylization and realism. The art of mime must be stylized, for it is an art which recreates and transposes. But reality is at its very base, and in the manner of translating the subject which is portrayed. The art of mime must therefore be realistic, as this stylization analyzes and translates objects and people who are real.[9]

Here Marceau distorts the traditional vocabulary of the theater. What he defines as realism is far from the conventional concept. Certainly he is not dealing with psychological realism; he is saying merely that the subjects, objects, and characters portrayed by the mime, find their origin in the real world. Theater of any style must use reality as a departure point. Stylization, which Marceau finds to be the translator of reality, is, in fact, precisely what prevents his mime from being considered realistic.

What is significant is Marceau's concern with the rendering of reality. Thus for him, mime is a representational form, totally reliant upon the successful creation of the illusion of something concrete. However, this illusion is not created through what is traditionally considered realistic technique, but is instead the result of stylization and exaggeration. Therefore, if Marceau's work were to be observed at close range, it would be evident that the literal gesture he performs is not equivalent to the real gesture one would make to "perform" the identical "verb" in every day life. It is a synopsis of gesture; it is Decroux's *raccourci* in action.

In a documentary on Marceau's work, *The Mime of Marcel Marceau*, this technique becomes quite clear.[10] Marceau demonstrates to his students how to perform the verb "to fold." He does a series of movements with his hands that have little to do with the real act of folding, but as the camera moves away, the illusion of folding is created. Distance clarifies the image created by the *raccourci*. That is why Marceau's craft works well in the large theaters and concert halls in which he often appears.

Thus, Marceau's style is similar to that of the impressionist painters. The lines and shapes are ill-defined, but the sense of the total form is clear. Through the use of *raccourcis*, Marceau creates the illusion or impression of the real. Although the movements are abbreviated, one has the sense of seeing the entire action. Marceau's art, like that of the impressionists, is less concerned with what is seen than with how one actually sees it. Therefore, the substance of his art is created by "the rapidity of his metamorphosis."[11]

Marceau affirms that the nineteenth-century caricaturists and impressionists are the two schools of painting that influenced his art the most. "The mime, after all, is nothing but a series of impressions," he says.[12] His acknowledgment of these influences is the key to an understanding of his work, which is a unique combination of impressionism and caricature. In many ways, Marceau's style is similar to nineteenth-century pantomime with its stock characters, exaggerated style, comic thrust, poetic mood, and mass appeal.

Marceau's mime requires that the audience translate mimic

gesture into its real life counterpart. There is thus a mime language into which the tangible elements of reality can be encoded. This language is based on the Decroux *grammaire*, which postulated translations for verbs into specific movements. The Marceau technique is based upon his personal adaptation of the Decroux code.

> Mime is the art of symbols. In the Webster[13] art of the mime, they amount to a system of conventions whereby the component parts of reality are broken down and stylized. Familiar gestures are identified by the public, though subservient to certain aesthetic rules. Style in the art of mime of western countries is the counterpart of symbols in far-eastern dancing. Some of these we have borrowed. . . . It is an art of illusion, blossoming under a magnetic spell, since the audience identifies itself with the characters on display, and even with the very *trickery* of it. [Emphasis added.][14]

Marceau believes that the mime tricks the audience into seeing the "nothing there." Although he claims that the public identifies with the characters, if his theory is followed logically, it is more likely that the audience role is to identify who or what the character is. For in fact, Marceau's audience is constantly involved in an active recognition process by which they decode the mime language into a literal one. Thus the success of a performance depends on active participation by the public. Understanding this interaction, Marceau plays to the public. Although Decroux used much the same basic technique, his performances failed, because he refused to recognize the reciprocal responsibility between mime and audience. His antagonistic attitude toward his public was antithetical to their role of interpreter, in which they must become the accomplice of the performer. Marceau's understanding of this involvement gives his art its popular appeal.

In summary, Marceau's performance process is as follows: By using the early Decroux technique, notably the *raccourci* and the *contrepoids,* Marceau creates a variety of illusions in his pantomimes, i.e., wind, distance, height. The titles held up before each number allow the audience to situate the exercise in order to play a silent guessing game, in which the objective is to identify the action and character being portrayed. As there is no real plot to most of these pantomimes, the fascination for the audience is in the challenge. It is Marceau's role to facilitate this recognition process through the fidelity with which he recreates the tangible world. Therefore the mime must display great virtuosity of movement in order to increase the likelihood of successful recognition by the public. Marceau's art thus depends on the perfection of technique.

> Gestures and attitudes in their natural state are ambiguous. When observing from afar two men fighting in the street, at first sight, one does not know if they are fighting in fun, or if it is for real. But the art of the mime erases ambiguity through stylization, still giving the audience a small margin for personal interpretation. One of the pleasures of the mime audience is that it is also a translator.[15]

Marceau has undertaken a dual role. On the one hand, he is the performer and challenger, presenting abstractions of reality to the audience for decoding; on the other, he presents these abstractions in a way that enables the audience to interpret them; he is also their coach. He "presents the abstraction of movement simply enough to be recognized and followed by everyone."[16] Marceau's wide audience appeal lies in his ability to draw the audience into his game. The public is fascinated by their mutual success. It is therefore to Marceau's advantage not to get into the realm of the abstract, nor to deal with complex themes. For ". . . in our naive pleasure in Marceau's art, we appreciated most easily what might be thought of as his conjuring tricks, his illusions of inanimate objects, and his stylization of the commonplace."[17]

Marceau's art is audience-oriented. By basing his success upon active participation by the public, he has revived mime as a popular art. Although he uses the Decroux techniques, his mime is closer in tone to the nineteenth-century pantomime, with its mass appeal. Marceau has achieved a unique combination of twentieth-century abstract movement with nineteenth-century mood. A critic remarks:

> I am grateful to Marcel Marceau and his company for bringing to light the true nobility of a dramatic genre which was running the risk of falling into oblivion through sterile reveries. It should be remembered that the Deburau Pantomimes which united with enthusiasm a diverse public, were conceived to be large enough to hold all the elements of that public, yet still were executed with the necessary technical

demands being met. Marcel Marceau possesses this technical strength.[18]

To capture this popular audience, Marceau, unlike Barrault and Decroux, emphasizes the comic, for he is aware of its appeal. In fact, his most lucid theorizing occurs on this topic. His lecture demonstrations, which charm the audience, showcase his pointed sense of humor. He explains how to create the comic effect. With his nose in the air, he portrays the haughty snob walking across the stage. At the peak of his smugness, he trips and loses grip of his self-assured presence. "This is how you make the public laugh," proclaims Marceau.[19] It is a humor of contrasts that he demonstrates, requiring caricature and exaggeration on both ends. If he did not portray an exaggeratedly smug personality, his downfall would be less humorous by contrast. This is not an original concept; it is a restatement of the classic slipping on a banana peel humor, but Marceau has mastered its implementation. "Bip's actions provoke laughter when they fail," he tells us.[20] So he plays up the comic element in Bip's impotence. He can also create suspense, instill fear in the audience, and then punctuate the moment of ultimate fright with comedy.[21] The audience is so relieved that the laugh is automatic. Exaggeration and contrast, these are the methods of Marceau.

In his search for the comic effect, Marceau must sacrifice sincerity of emotion. He demonstrates how a realistic actor would smell a flower and then how a mime would do the same thing. "The sincere actor breathes in the fragrance of the flower in a realistic manner: The mime brings the flower to his nose in a sweeping grandiose gesture, smells the flower, and then he wilts from the bad odor."[22] Once again, we see the comedy of contrast in action. Marceau gives the audience the opposite of what they expect, but first he sets them up through the sweeping poetic gesture—counterpoint—the nonpoetic stench. This brings surprise and then laughter. Note that Marceau himself compares this to the work of the "sincere actor," for his concern for the broad comic effect, realized through caricature, is antithetical to the tenets of psychological realism.

In an interview Marceau stated, "I work with a mirror."[23] This brings to mind the passage from Stanislavski in which he cautions:

You must be very careful in the use of a mirror. It teaches the actor to watch the outside rather than the inside of his soul. . . . Consequently, while you were working with the mirror, what interested you was not so much your exterior, your general appearance, your gestures, but principally the way in which you externalized your inner sensations. . . . You fixed these methods of expressing your feelings in a permanent form. . . . Then in the end you worked out a definite external form for the interpretation of certain successful parts in your role, and you were always able to achieve their external expression through technique.[24]

Here Stanislavski is criticizing the young actor for his external preparation—yet this method seems an accurate description of Marceau's system. For years he has repeated perfectly externalized patterns, using a mirror and reaching character only through action.[25] When "Marcel Marceau brought pantomime to this continent's attention, it looked like excellent sense memory, a closing of the gap between movement and the actor, but investigation revealed its technique. Pantomime, too, was external."[26] Marceau justifies the external emphasis of mime:

What is difficult is to create psychological situations which are explained only by body involvement, with grace, with poetry and clarity. It requires virtuosity of the body, complete understanding of what man plans to do. You eat a piece of cake, that's obvious, even if it's done with style. But to express feeling—the problem of death, life, solitude—through mime, through concrete symbols, that is difficult.[27]

Recognizing the difficulty of expressing interior states with the techniques of objective mime, Marceau chooses to invert the Stanislavski method.

It would thus appear that Marceau is not seeking emotional authenticity for his characters, that his primary concern is caricature and technique, through which he achieves the comic effect. However, he often makes the claim that he is creating characters with which his audience can identify.[28] This implies that Marceau's goals may be in opposition to his technique: that he may not achieve the development of character he desires. This disparity will be demonstrated in the analysis of his Bip numbers.

It is therefore interesting that when Marceau uses the term *mime subjectif,* which for Barrault was the basis for character work, he is using it in a different sense than Barrault was:

> We distinguish between pure mechanical movements which are born of objects: *mime objectif,* and those movements which touch the character and passions of the human being, those which equally grow out of the identification of one's self with all the elements, which we call *le mime subjectif.*[29]

For Marceau the subjective mime is external.

When Barrault developed this concept, he intended it to express "the metaphysical attitude of man in space." As such, it was the basis for his concept of *le mime tragique.* Marceau's use of the term indicates that his idea of tragedy is not akin to that of Barrault. This statement by Marceau reveals the disparity between the two men on this point: "Buffoonery is close to a certain kind of tragedy . . . the extreme openness of Bip can be both comic and serious, because Bip is a sinking soul, hooked to the real world only through sentiment."[30] Thus for Marceau, tragedy is linked to sentimentality, to the melodramatic aspects of existence that can be portrayed externally. The unhappy is equal to the tragic. For Barrault, tragedy deals with the conflict between the inner man and his environment, realized only through character development and unification of psyche and action.

As their respective concepts of the tragic differ, their attitudes toward the comic vary accordingly. Early in Marceau's career, many critics applauded this divergence from his illustrious predecessor. Referring to Barrault's *mime tragique,* they had this to say:

> Mime was, and had to be, obligatorily tragic and obscure. Above all the comic and burlesque elements which risked vulgarity had to be deleted, thus never could mime be refined and ambiguous enough in the minutest detail.[31]

> Marcel Marceau did not listen to the arguments of his great, but temporary master [Barrault], and Marceau was right.[32]

Marceau and the critics ignored Barrault's admonitions that "one should eliminate the comic and burlesque from mime."[33] Barrault insisted on this point, for he knew it is a short step from the zenith of tragedy over the precipice to comic puerility. Barrault was not against the use of comedy per se, but against the patronizing use of the comic. One critic warned of the hazards on both ends:

> The danger is there: In the quest for the comic effect one risks making too many concessions to the public. . . . There is a contradictory danger in the quest for the symbolic, in the over-refinement of style which tends to be too cerebral.[34]

Despite the perils of going to an extreme in either direction, Marceau, with his strong commercial sense, has clearly opted for the comic and burlesque alternative. In doing so "he is often caught up in the puerile, and in superficial mugging,"[35] claims one critic. His whiteface facilitates this facial expression, and is a point of divergence from Decroux.

One critic, in considering Marceau's roots, finds it strange that he has chosen this course:

> It is curious to note that this student of Decroux's school— through which Barrault has passed—finds his inspiration in broad subjects, that his sense of humor depends on the "gag."[36]

This is not an inexplicable phenomenon. It is a function of Marceau's personality and goals. The public thrives on the gag, and so Marceau uses it to his advantage. Decroux, uninterested in public acclaim, was not intrigued by this form of humor. Barrault's view of the role of mime left the feeling that the gag cheapened an art that could be noble. But Marceau, the courter of the public, despite his training with these two men, turns to the gag. It is a form of humor that flows from Marceau's natural sense of timing. Some critics believe Marceau discovered this kind of comedy in American silent films.[37]

Despite the use of the gag, most of Marceau's work is antithetical to the style used in silent films. The cinema has traditionally been a realistic medium. Certainly the silent films made no attempt at abstraction. The reality that exists in films is concrete and tangible. The world of Marceau is imaginary. R. G. Davis has made an interesting comparison of the styles of Chaplin, whom he calls the mime, and Marceau, whom he calls the pantomimist.

The Pantomimist	The Mime
Closer to dance	Closer to drama
Usually masked and mute	Can speak and sing
Moves to music	Moves to act
Dealing with	Using
"nothing there" he must communicate his prop to tell his story	tangible props he exhorts and manipulates their symbolism to comment on the story
Charmed	Stimulated
the viewer guesses "What does he have there?"	the viewer thinks "What does what he has there mean?"[38]

Marceau, according to Davis, does not explore multiple meaning levels, but exposes a story line in silent language that must be decoded by the audience. Davis continues:

> Chaplin works with tangibles—hat, flower, cane, folding Murphy bed—articles that are transformed into symbols in a dramatic relationship. Once in his hands, a prop is itself plus the entire dramatic potential of "prop to Chaplin." . . . In every instance the real prop is his point of contact and departure—the dance of the rolls in *Gold Rush,* of the wrenches in *Modern Times,* each a creative variation employed symbolically toward statement and abstraction. . . .
> Marceau deals with "nothing there."[39]

Sensing the shift of emphasis in film, Marceau states,

> We are living in a period of realism. We have today something special, the movies. . . . If I work in a film, I must do mime, but I need to change my style.[40]

An important distinction between the two techniques is that Chaplin considers himself to be, above all, a character actor,[41] while Marceau sees himself as a caricaturist in the manner of Daumier. This difference is a significant one, affecting the style and dimension of Marceau's work. Interestingly enough, despite the obvious variances in style and technique, Marceau says that Chaplin inspired him to become a mime.[42] Because Marceau does not deal with interior character development, whereas Chaplin does, Davis, in devising the chart comparing mime and pantomime, placed the former's art closer to dance and the latter closer to drama. However, Marceau believes there is a clear distinction between what he does and dance:

> Dance bases movement on footsteps, mime deals with metamorphosis in man, and the identification of man with the elements. It is the art of transformation. It is slow motion, attached to the ground, more earthly than dance. Mime does use many ballet movements. When mime wants to express gaiety it goes toward dance, but while dance moves quickly in steps, mime strikes a symbolic attitude, is clean and more brief. Every gesture has significance. Mime makes a statement from a convention you recognize in life. Dance need not have meaning, it needs only to be beautiful. . . .
>
> Some things may be expressed in the same way, and today's great ballet employs much mime, but generally mime is more elliptic, shorter, and more condensed than dance. . . .[43]

The condensation of movement to which he refers is the essence of the *raccourci*. In his comparison between mime and dance, Marceau has defined the *raccourci* that he uses so effectively. Marceau is also expressing what Decroux labeled the Promethean aspect of mime—its earthliness. Marceau continues his comparison:

> Mime can choose a beautiful subject in the same way as ballet, but it is more like sculpture than dance. In modern ballet Martha Graham has occasionally gone back to Greek sculpture for inspiration. When she does this she approaches mime. The two forms, mime and dance, can resemble each other while remaining entirely different. Mime, through attitudes, gives the feeling of action. Dance gives action to feeling.[44]

Here, Marceau is referring to the *mime statuaire,* one of the basic concepts of the Decroux grammar. Martha Graham often contradicts the classic weightless concept of dance—the idea of the dancer on her points, reaching upward, or the gravity-defying leaps. In a piece such as *Lamentations,* she performs more than half of the dance seated, with the basic movements being changes in the spinal column. It is this earthliness of Martha Graham that brings her close to mime's solid sculptural forms.

Marceau claims that "while dance exalts and ascends harmonically upon music, mime supports its intensity with silence."[45] Yet is is interesting that he uses background music, and does not depend on silence. Marceau implies here that the role of music is different in mime from that in dance, but he is unclear as to the exact discrepancy in function. He states, "Mime, too, can make use of music. The public accepts music as it gives the gesture a certain density. Music can be a counter-point."[46] This suggests that music, although not intrinsic to mine, can add to its expressive quality, not as rhythmic support as in dance, but as a foil for movement, or to create a mood.

Thus Marceau's analysis of the division between mime and dance is an echo of Decroux's ideas on the subject. There is one significant divergence between the two: Marceau sees a creative role for music, which he believes does not detract from cor-poral expression but, on the contrary, enhances it.

Marceau differs from Barrault and Decroux in his concep-tual approach to mime. He is not a theoretician but a prac-titioner. Far from the analytical Decroux, when Marceau was asked how he analyzed an action into its essential parts, he replied, "It can't be explained; it is accomplished by tech-nique."[47] When he does attempt explanations, they are often riddled with inconsistence in terminology. But Marceau makes no error in his application of the technique. He has perfected, refined, and adapted the new mime to his personal needs.

Marceau's first performances after he left Barrault were *mimodrames*, "plays with neither words nor music, where the dramatic action gels solely out of the relationship the mimes establish silently among themselves."[48] This form is rooted in the Deburau tradition. The *Théâtre du Boulevard,* the nineteenth-century people's theater, used this genre almost ex-clusively. Marceau's concern for audience involvement made this style most appealing, as its gestural language is "universal and quickly understood."[49] He thus set out to revive the tradi-tion of the *pantomime blanche.*

The hallmark of pantomime in France was the Pierrot character, which reached the zenith of its development with Deburau. Recognizing the historical significance of this figure, Marceau attempts to resuscitate him. He explains:

> This Pierrot, the key character in the art of mime, presented under so many guises by Deburau, Severin, Wague, Jean-Louis Barrault, was abandoned on the Boulevard of Crime. I wanted to revive him. Preserving the essential characteristics

of classical pantomime, and placing him in the period of Daumier and Lautrec.[50]

Marceau saw the members of his troupe as the stock characters of the old pantomime rooted in the Commedia tradition: Cassandra, Colombine, Arlequin, Policinelle and Pirrette were revived. Marceau claimed for himself the character of Pierrot. But Marceau's Pierrot differed greatly from the great Deburau version. Marceau sees him more in the late nineteenth-century romantic form: "Pierrot goes through life with the continual hope for better times."[51] Hence the drama of Pierrot for Marceau is that of the poet, the creature of fantasy who is always at odds with reality.

Although Marceau produced many *mimodrames* from 1947 to 1964, an examination of his three most celebrated works will create an image of this genre.[52]

Mort avant l'aube, the first of the *mimodrames,* which won for him the *Prix Deburau* in 1948, deals directly with the Pierrot theme. When the curtain opens, we see the principal character, Ghoé, hanging from a street lamp. He comes back to life to tell us his sad story.

> Life was against him, bad luck at every turn; so he dreams he can conquer this life of his. But when the night is done, and the beams of moonlight die, he hangs himself before dawn. . . . All of this takes place as in a dream, like a black and white drawing, as in a short symbolic poem. Pure mime is wedded with pure poetry. . . .[53]

The concept of the poetic soul at odds with his environment is a direct descendant of the black Pierrots of the late nineteenth century. This lyric, romantic mimodrame shows Marceau's link to that tradition. However, while the thematic material belonged to the era of the black Pierrots, the staging was a pastiche of several styles. There were oversized expressionistic masks worn atop black costumes against a black backdrop, creating the ghostlike impression of disembodied characters floating in the night. There was a modern abstract set of white silhouettes painted against the black. In a total break from the silent Deburau tradition, Roger Blin narrated the story of Ghoé as the actors mimed the action. This narrative element indicates that Marceau still relied on text. The stylization and use of multiple effects and text is reminiscent of *Autour d'une mère,* but whereas Barrault dealt with the primitive expression of the naked body, relying on character development and a visceral quality that integrated sound with movement, Marceau's style was more consciously refined. Text was an accoutrement to movement occurring in external narration; masks, props, and costumes supported the gestural language.

Le manteau, inspired by a Gogol short story, once again expresses the Pierrot theme. Here, a young clerk dreams of owning a fur coat to replace his tattered garment. For years he works overtime to save enough money to attain this goal. At long last he buys the coat of his dreams, and with it he acquires dignity and respect from his friends and a whole new sense of self. He is invited out for a night on the town by his admiring friends. On the way home he is attacked by a band of robbers, who steal his treasured fur and, with it, his newfound status and future dreams. Society's underdog suffers again. One reviewer called it "a series of characters from an outdated existentialism,"[54] but this seems to be a misinterpretation of the Gogol story and of Marceau's philosophy of tragedy. If *Le Manteau* is outdated, it is not because of its existential quality, but because of its nineteenth-century romantic nature. Marceau describes his goals:

> Imagine the fantastic grayness of the everyday world of Gogol set against the colorful world of Montmartre. Using mime to tell this story is justified by the form's ability to, on the one hand, amuse and move the audience, and on the other, its ability to portray the grotesque and tragic aspects of existence. The scrutiny of these elements is the very essence of drama. It was this contrast which inspired me to revive *Le Manteau.*[55]

The style of *Le Manteau* was similar to that of *Mort avant l'aube.* It, too, appeared like a black-and-white Daumier drawing. Once again, Marceau played the role of the lyric character pitted against a chorus of functionaries and bureaucrats.

When Marceau's *mimodrames* were not romantic vignettes, they were celebratory fantasies such as *La Foire,* "a sort of ballet of automatons, played by the entire cast, all decked out in masks and gaudy costumes."[56] Here Marceau portrayed the gaiety and excitement of a fair, with his cast playing both the carnival entertainers and the admiring public. Later, in his style pantomimes, he extracted some of the elements from this pantomime, which was apparently a series of short mimed circus acts. These gave Marceau a pretext for demonstrating the Decroux technique. In this mimodrame Marceau used all the accoutrements of the stage: costumes, colorful sets, music, and weird recorded sound effects blasted over speakers. This can be directly contrasted to his performances today, which occur, for all practical purposes, on a bare stage and with only minimal musical accompaniment.

These three examples are typical of the romantic lyric style of the mimodrames. Marceau tells us that there were two criteria that all the *mimodrames* had to meet: "unity in the characters and simplicity in the theme. The pantomimes could be comic or burlesque, but they were always dramatic, and above all social."[57] From 1948–1956 Marceau divided his performances between his solo numbers as Bip, and the *mimodrames*. On the whole, the *mimodrames* were less warmly received by the critics. There were many occasions on which the critics badly panned the ensemble part of his performance:

> He will pardon me if I confess that I liked the mimodrames so much less than the rest of the performance. They were more conventional, more pretentious, and each one was at least three times too long.[58]

> . . . *The Overcoat*, which while adroitly using mimetic techniques, only did what drama or the short story could do better.[59]

> One finds himself persuaded that the reach of pantomime action can be more vast and more varied.[60]

There seems to be a repeated criticism that the mimodrames were too contrived:

> He [Marceau] finds himself far away from pantomime which is an intuitive art, something he does not understand. He finds only one solution: to enlarge and exaggerate, to transform intuition into affirmation; this is the exercise which is brutally accomplished by la companie Marcel Marceau.[61]

> . . . the idea comes before gesture, emotion is fragmented in an artificial manner, where everything is affirmed at length, taking great pains to satisfy the spirit before touching the heart.
> In brief, I reproach Marceau for having given himself up

to intelligence, and at that a literary intelligence, which can hardly be fitting when attempting to reach a public which does not want reasons but sensitivity. This sensitivity bursts out when Marceau is master of the stage, but as soon as he withdraws, he cedes his place to actors too much under the domination of ballet mechanics. It is all very well done, but it doesn't have enough sincerity, enough flesh and blood.[62]

This criticism suggests that the mimodrames were not as readily appreciated as the solo numbers by the modern audiences. This can be attributed to several factors. Marceau took a nineteenth-century genre but used modern mimetic techniques. The *raccourci,* the abstraction of movement, appears contrived against the simple romantic background. On the other hand, the form of the mimodrames is naturalistic. It uses props, costumes, and a naturalistic time-space continuum. The contemporary audience is accustomed to seeing psychologically developed characters functioning against such a setting. Thus whether viewed from the nineteenth- or twentieth-century perspective, the mimodrames had anachronistic elements. Marceau has acknowledged that he does not create the interior character, and it has been demonstrated that his methods are antithetical to the development of emotional authenticity. The interaction of superficially drawn caricatures against a realistic situation gave the impression of overexaggeration and shallowness. For this reason the critics accused the *mimodrames* of lacking sincerity. Actually, they lacked no more emotional authenticity than Marceau's other numbers, which are also intellectual and contrived. But the realistic setting, coupled with the presence of many actors on the stage, magnified these factors. It provided the same effect as the film in creating a naturalistic background for Marceau's style, which he has acknowledged must be modified for the cinematic context.

This comment helps to explain the *mimodrame*'s relative lack of success:

The mime puts into action very different forces if he plays alone or if he acts with a troupe.

If he plays alone, he creates the magic alone. He becomes plant, fish, object. When Marceau walks against the wind he creates the wind. . . .

When the mime acts with a troupe, a part of the magic is

destroyed, or at the very least it is spread over the various characters.[63]

This indicates that the realistic context prevents the creation of the illusion of reality, the magic trick upon which Marceau's art is based. Since his craft is so clearly based on virtuosity of movement, the ensemble performance diminishes the awesome quality of his technique by changing the context and focus of the performance.

When asked why he did not abandon the *mimodrames* and limit himself to Bip numbers, Marceau answered, "To play Bip would be to do virtuoso work. I need the anxiety of the theatre, the machinery, the lights."[64] But the logistical problems of touring with a large company pushed Marceau to abandon his troupe, and he has since made only solo performances.

Thus from 1956 to the present, his performances have been divided between Bip adventures and the *pantomimes de style*.

The *pantomimes de style* represent an ensemble of exercises of corporal virtuosity. They were originally created to astound the public with a pure and ancient, but forgotten form. The anecdote served only as a pretext, for the goal was to establish a dramatic language which would establish the autonomy of mime from other plastic arts.[65]

This "dramatic language" was that of the original Decroux grammaire. But the anecdote that transformed the analytic exercises of the Decroux code into entertaining pieces was the personal creative contribution of Marceau.

Marceau has over thirty style pantomimes in his repertoire. They share many things in common: scrupulous use of the *contrepoids* and the *raccourci*, totally controlled movement, use of caricature and the gag for the comic effect or sentimentality and melodrama for the serious. Each number is always preceded by a title card. Marceau performs them all in the same costume: white jumpsuit with horizontally striped top, and ballet slippers. His makeup is the whiteface of the *pantomime blanche*.

As indicated by their titles, *Walking, Walking Against the Wind, The 1500 Meter, The Staircase, The Tight Rope Walker,* and *The Kite,* are designed to be demonstrations of the virtuoso technique with which Marceau renders the Decroux code. But through the use of caricature and the gag, Marceau adds another dimension. In a number such as *The Tight Rope Walker,* instead of merely creating the illusion of the high wire through walking in the studied manner of the aerialist, he presents, along with the physical demonstration, a portrayal of the emotions of the acrobat, i.e., fear, insecurity, self-satisfaction. He implements his theory of the comedy of contrast: Just as the tightrope walker thinks he has performed a great stunt and is basking in the satisfaction of his accomplishment, Marceau has him lose his balance to create a humorous counterpoint. In *The Staircase,* he gives the illusion of ascent using the same Decroux technique Barrault implemented in *La Faim.* But whereas for the latter it was just a small effect in a larger theatrical piece, for Marceau the illusion is the ultimate goal of the number. He maintains audience attention by turning the staircase into a metaphor for insurmountable problems and adding the comic effect.

Other numbers are pretexts for Marceau to draw caricatures through movement. *The Public Garden* is most representative of this form. Here he presents action portraits of various characters walking in a park. Old ladies on a bench become cackling gossips, the man walking his dog becomes a pretext for a tug-of-war on an imaginary leash where Marceau can demonstrate the power of the *contrepoids.* Similar technique is used to render the vendor of balloons—helium-filled of course, so there can be a struggle against the upward pull of the gas. Strolling lovers are exaggeratedly romantic and self-involved. The mother pushing the baby carriage becomes a doting, overly protective, excited new mother. Other characters are drawn in much the same manner. No park scene would be complete without the statue that comes to life and gives Marceau's sketch a romantic, lyric quality. During this number, the public attempts to guess who each character is and what he or she is doing, enthralled as Marceau makes the invisible visible.

Marceau understands the importance of injecting recognizable human and social elements into his work, for it is this aspect of his art that keeps the audience involved in the guessing game they must play.

> People have to identify themselves with what I am doing. I have to present problems which I have in everyday life, or which they are facing themselves. I have to present a satire

on things which everyone has shared in his life. If there's no identification, there's no rapport with the public.[66]

The humor and appeal of these pantomimes lies in Marceau's ability to create audience identification of and with these human attributes.

Here the most significant difference between Decroux and Marceau becomes clear. Decroux created the mime grammar, the language of gestures that permits Marceau to create so effectively the illusion of walking in place, upstairs, against the wind, etc., but when Decroux performed, he could do nothing more than the demonstration. He repudiated the elements of humor and characterization. Once the intrigue of the illusion wore off, there was nothing to hold the attention of an audience of non-mimes, as they were not interested in an analytic demonstration of the techniques, but in being entertained. This is why Decroux remains a mime's mime.

Marceau is the illusionist. He has used the word magic to describe what he does, but he has learned what every good magician knows, that even a series of meticulously executed tricks will not hold an audience unless accompanied by showmanship, bravura, humor, and human interest. He extracts these elements from the popular tradition of mime and pantomime.

The style pantomimes developed, becoming technically and thematically more complex. There was an attempt to link technique to poetic imagery and universal themes. *The Maskmaker* is one such work. Here Marceau depicts the drama of a maskmaker trapped in a mask of his own creation. This becomes an obvious poetic metaphor for the role playing in life that often holds us prisoner. Marceau comments:

I wanted to show not the tragic mask, but the moment of solitude of man where once in his life he confronts the reality of himself. Society puts on so many masks, but what is the real mask of us, the mask of our soul? I wanted to show the real bare face. My own mask is that I laugh as everyone does when he goes through emotional situations. But in "The Maskmaker" it becomes a symbol when the funny mask is taken off, and suddenly man realizes the moment of truth, which is to be oneself completely. *Dépouillment,* bareness. It is like death and birth. The end of something and the start.[67]

It is interesting that Marceau has found a means to turn a tool of his own trade—the mask—into a symbol. The mask-maker trying on various masks becomes the pretext for a virtuoso demonstration of facial exercises. Once again Marceau finds a way to combine technique with a dramatic situation.

The following passage gives insight into how Marceau achieves his unique effects:

> Every part of the body is important: the face, neck, the trunk, the hands, the feet. Through the hands you can create a sort of transposition of elements: snakes, butterflies. You can create love—the touch. Through the feet you give the image of space through moving, of how the mime dominates the elements. . . . In slow motion he has to show the tragedy and comedy of man. He is torn between death and life, sky and earth.[68]

This passage indicates how Marceau recounts the story of Genesis in *The Creation of the World,* with only the measured movements of his body. Here the hands become the tempting serpent, and then are miraculously transformed into Eve's caressing arms. Love is given through the touch. Marceau manages to play man and woman simultaneously through using different parts of his body to represent each sex. The torso remains male, the hands and arms female. The feet create the sense of time and space. They establish man's relationship with the world.

Youth, Maturity, Old Age and Death depicts the cycle of human life. In three minutes, Marceau takes the audience through a lifetime. He starts in near fetal position, rises toward the strength of youth with its attitude of exuberance, to the erect control of middle age, toward old age and the gradual sinking inward of the body, till the immobility of death. Upon careful examination of the torso during this number, it is evident that Marceau breaks down the barriers of time through subtle changes in the spine and pelvis. In youth, the chest is thrust forward as if asserting an open attitude toward life. The back must arch to achieve this. In maturity, the spine is straight, the direction clear. In old age, the back hunches, the torso bends forward. In death, the support of the spine disappears. By keeping the movement fluid, Marceau gives the sense of a continuous process. The feet and arms support the posture of the torso. The entire number is done to a constant walk in place, with an accompanying swing of the arms. This constant movement creates the sense of the passage of time. The degree of hand movement indicates the activity of each age of man. It is the cessation of such movement that spells death. Thus the limbs resound the central posture of the torso—this becomes a perfected application of Decroux's *mime statuaire* with its emphasis on the attitude of the torso, and complement of the limbs. This number is merely a scale around the vertebral column, extracted directly from the Decroux *gymnastique,* but applied in Marceau's personal style with added dimension and meaning.

The Cage plays upon thematic material similar to *The Maskmaker.* Once again, man is seen as being trapped, only this time inside a cage. Once again, the metaphor is obvious. This time Marceau relies upon effective use of the *contrepoids* to portray the desperate attempts at escape. The cage is created through counterbalancing the resistance of the walls as they close slowly in. Just when freedom has been obtained and jubilation prevails, another cage appears. Despite the seriousness of the theme, Marceau draws humor out of the moment of reentrapment, for it presents the comic contrast of emotional states. But the comedy is short-lived as the cell becomes smaller and smaller, offering no hope for survival. The prisoner appears to diminish in size as well. Through subtle changes in the spinal column, he shrinks, emphasizing his impotency.

The Creation of the World, The Mask Maker, Youth, Maturity, Old Age and Death, and *The Cage* are representative of the more complex style pantomimes. But the basic structure of all of them remains the same. Impeccable implementation of the early Decroux technique, coupled with elements for audience appeal: humor, caricature, poetic images, social commentary. Marceau devotes the first half of his program to the *pantomimes de style.* For the remainder of his performance he portrays the adventures of Bip.

As mentioned above, in 1947, Marceau created, a character who would serve as a vehicle for mime expression, a new Pierrot whom he baptized Bip after the character Pip in Dickens's *Great Expectations.* He states, "Before devoting myself to my mimodrames I needed to create a *personnage.* I could not repeat Chaplin or Pierrot, and so I thought of Pip, a hero of Dickens."[69] Apparently Marceau liked the novel, the innocence of the character, and the sound of the name, but there is nothing in the story of how he made his choice to indicate any hint of a resemblance between the two characters beyond the obvious homonymous one. Far from the Pip of Dickens, Marceau describes his character as "the successor of the Greek and Roman mimes, such as Pylades and Roescus, those of the middle ages, or of the Italian players, Brighella's or Pietrolino's little cousin, but closer to the Pierrots of the nineteenth century."[70] Bip was to serve as Marceau's persona.

Marceau consciously created the physical Bip, making him a pastiche of the classical mime characters:

> My eyebrows are too close together, which can give a hard look to the face. To seem more naive, I drew false eyebrows very high, about two or three centimeters above mine. Instead of using the straight eyebrows of Pierrot, I made them the circumflex shape of Arlequin, which can become cynical.
>
> I also revolutionized the mouth. The traditional Pierrot had a red, round, effeminate mouth. I made a straight mouth, and then traced the outline in black.[71]
>
> I use the white face to make Bip symbolic . . . I can represent somebody ageless and sexless . . . universal.[72]

Marceau thus consciously adapted the traits of the classic Pierrot and stock Commedia characters to his own needs, at the same time attempting to make Bip the heir apparent to that tradition.

Marceau proclaims, "Bip is a twentieth century Pierrot, with him I can create a new style of mime using his adventures."[73] This statement raises several questions:
1. Is Bip really part of the Pierrot tradition?
2. Is there something distinctive about Bip that makes him a creature of the twentieth century?
3. Has Marceau created a "new style of mime" through him?

In answer to the first question, if Duchartre and Nicoll are correct in tracing the French Pierrot back to the Commedia Pagliaccio, Pedrolino and Piero, then Bip does not appear as the heir to that family of clowns for he is not like the Commedia characters.[74] Their gestures were more fixed, their personalities more clearly drawn. They were more active, often mischievous; the valet types from Brighella to Pedrolino maneuvered people, were manipulators of situations. Although they were often victimized zanies, they tended to create many of their own problems. Bip is more passive. He seems to be the eternal victim; things happen to him. The Pierrot of Deburau, in the early nineteenth century, had much more spunk and personality. Marceau wants Bip to be the symbol of the people, but Deburau's Pierrot was the voice of the people. Deburau turned his Pierrot into a malicious hero of the masses. Bip merely represents their impotence. The traditional clown character used acrobatics as a primary means of expression. Large sweeping movements were usual. But Marceau uses studied distilled movements, stylized and refined. There is not the élan of the earlier characters. Bip is really closer to the melodramatic black Pierrot of the late nineteenth century, that of Le Grand, Wague, and Severin who brought Pierrot toward the literary tradition.[75] For these were sentimental lyric clowns, and "Bip, lunary character, despite everything, belongs more to the abstract world of poetry than to the classical school of corporal movement and expression."[76] Thus Bip is part of the Pierrot tradition, but he has most in common with the Pierrot that represents the decline of that style. He shares few of the traits associated with the heights the character attained under the auspices of Deburau.

In answer to the second question, is Bip a twentieth-century character, Bip is the epitome of social impotence. He is the eternal victim of circumstances beyond his own control. He is the incurable romantic who dreams of what might have been or what could be. He is the naive child in the process of discovering the world. Marceau expounds on Bip the victim:

If Bip, the rope-puller makes the audience laugh, it is because he is the constant victim of the other team of rope-pullers, the invisible, suggested all-powerful team—the *contrepoids*. If "Bip at the Society Party" makes people laugh, it is because he is the victim of society's invisible, suggested, all-powerful *contrepoids*. The mime in modern times is the poor fellow who is out of the general scheme of things. This conflict is the condition of his existence. Bip is spirit. He has, as a *contrepoids*, matter. This is the drama which makes us laugh so much.[77]

And on Bip the romantic:

Watching, listening with a timid ear and a wistful face to the laughter, tears and applause of the people who identify themselves with him.[78]

But are these the qualities associated with a twentieth-century character? Despite Marceau's statement to that effect, Bip by his own description has all the qualities of the late nineteenth-century lyric Pierrot. Coupled with Bip's lack of inner psychological motivation, this makes Bip a questionable embodiment of the contemporary man.

It is an obvious temptation for the critics to compare Bip to Chaplin's little tramp—

> Bip, a Chaplinesque figure of his own creation is a sort of comic everyman, who, dressed in a striped pullover shirt, tight pants and battered stove-pipe hat with its pathetic little flower, parades in white face up and down the boulevards of the world. . . .[79]

However, the two have little in common. The Chaplin character is a fighter, a survivor, a little man with a social conscience who actively helps society's underlings although he is one of them himself. Marceau describes Bip as "pure spirit"[80] As such he is the perfect vehicle for the rendering of illusion, the primary goal of Marceau's art. Chaplin is more oriented toward the realization of social and political themes within a realistic context, and as such cannot use a character of such ephemeral nature.

In answer to the third question, has Marceau created a new style of mime using Bip's adventures, comparative analysis of the Bip and style pantomimes reveals that there is no fundamental difference in style or technique between the two forms. The makeup and costume remain virtually identical, with only one minor alteration:

> The only apparent difference between the "style" pantomimes and the "Bip" pantomimes is that in the latter Marceau enters wearing a corny tattered hat with a flower in it, which he promptly removes. Otherwise, the mime and his costume remain the same.[81]

Obviously, in the style pantomimes, Marceau can portray many characters: he can be all the people in the park; whereas, in the Bip numbers, he must always be Bip. But in terms of character development, despite Marceau's statement, there is no difference between the two forms. In both, "he works as a clown, first as a nonspecific clown and later as a clown character called

Bip."[82] But Bip himself, because of the lack of interior psychological development, is a nonspecific character, and is, in fact, another of Marceau's caricatures. Marceau continues to use mime technique in an identical fashion. For instance *Bip at a Society Party,* which portrays the misadventures of the clown out of his milieu, continues the use of the *contrepoids* to create the existence of the invisible. Bip leans against invisible walls, drinks from nonexistent glasses, spills imaginary soup. Thus Bip is merely another pretext for virtuoso demonstration of the Decroux technique. Developed in much the same way, *Bip Hunts Butterflies* recounts the story of Bip's confrontation with the ephemeral quality of the life of the butterfly, as he is left with the awesome responsibility of determining its fate. The captured butterfly is portrayed only through palpitating hand movements which suggest the flutter of the wings. Here Marceau uses the techniques of the style pantomimes in which the hands indicate a transposition of elements, just as they became the serpent in *Creation of the World.* Marceau creates the butterfly's flight through head movements which appear to follow its trajectory. The audience infers the movement of the butterfly from the external focus of Marceau's concentration.

Recently, Marceau added a new Bip routine that clearly demonstrates the basis of his art—*Bip, Illusionist.* As the title reveals, he casts his character in the role he himself has been playing for thirty years. It is a magic show, with Bip appearing everywhere on the stage at once. Through the use of trickery, he challenges the audience into asking, "How does he do it?" Although this is a recent creation, it appears to be a step backwards, for there is no meaning beyond the trick, no pretext for the illusion as there was in other numbers. There is even a diminution in technique, for he demonstrates little of his physical prowess here. It also undermines Marceau's concept of the significance of the Bip character, for it appears hardly necessary to have created what Marceau himself describes as "a poetic and burlesque hero of our times caught up in the contradictions of the modern world"[83] in order to play illusionist games with the audience.

Although Marceau uses impeccable technique to create the Bip adventures, the constant attempts at illusion prohibit this character from reaching the symbolic proportion Marceau would like him to attain as a modern Pierrot. He becomes instead a vehicle for virtuosity.

"Bip as a Lion Tamer," "Bip and the Rope," "The Bath," are excellent music-hall numbers, very adeptly staged, crafty, but which are on the sidelines of the great pantomime tradition. The dream is absent. The intangible world where phantoms and pure ideas hide has disappeared. . . . The strokes of the stick, and terrestrial truths have lost their tragic power. The cruel disillusionment, the naiveté and tenderness which painfully marked Barrault's face have vanished.[84]

All the Bip numbers share the essential elements of the style pantomimes. The technique is identical. They both use caricature and the gag for comic effect, and are lyric and sentimental when the mood is serious. In both cases, Marceau finds thematic and anecdotal pretexts to demonstrate virtuoso mime movement. Although Marceau describes Bip as a twentieth-century Pierrot through which he creates a new style, analysis of these numbers does not bear out these claims.

Recently, Marceau has performed on film and television, but his art does not translate easily into these media, which use the traditional trappings of realism. The goals of Marceau's work is to render visible the invisible, and this is antithetical to the nature of these forms, which portray tangible reality.

Mime is not the same on a T.V. screen. When Bip is in the open (on stage), the audience feels his presence, the projection of his personality. If I am hired to do T.V., I have to use props and it destroys what I do. I am a magician in a world where a magician is not needed.[85]

Here Marceau affirms his role as illusionist.

The mime, whose style requires caricature, enlargement, and exaggeration, must be very careful when transferring his work to the cinema, which is, in itself, a giant blowup of reality. This can create a double magnification resulting in distortion.

The gesture which can express an idea on the stage must be transposed for the screen, which magnifies it like a magnifying glass. The transposition occurs as a total reduction in construction; it must be compensated for and recomposed proportionately.[86]

Still, Marceau continues to do occasional film work, but he has never paralleled his stage success on the screen. In 1974, he made a feature film, *Shanks,* for Paramount Pictures. It was a box office disaster. This bizarre tale of a mad scientist who has found a means to mechanically reactivate corpses enabled Marceau to play a series of marionette characters (dead bodies wired as mechanized puppets). The story required the stylization of movement usually associated with Marceau's work, and the mood was reminiscent of a description of his early *mimodrames:*

> He struggles in a mysterious and closed world which is often hostile in its caricatures. This is the world of the mimodrame, so close to the world of marionettes through its disdain for human emotion.[87]

Although the plot enabled Marceau to work within his established style, he still had to contend with real props, real space, and other actors. This provided the same difficulties he experienced in his mimodrames. He could not achieve the magic effects of his stage performances. Confirmed a critic:

> Mr. Marceau, who has been seen in several films including *Barbarella,* does not achieve the remarkable illusions he has created on stage. . . .
> . . . the magic here is diffused. The succession of grim, cute or gimmicky approaches to this "fairy story" make it an extraordinary but only intermittently edifying fable.[88]

Marceau explains why he persists in performing in films despite his limited success in the medium:

> Of course, it is sometimes difficult in my work to see what effect I have while I am alive. But when I have created a style in a film and when I am dead they revive it, say in thirty, no forty years . . . then I will be unique. MARCEAU! Not like Bardot.[89]

Marceau thus hopes to achieve immortality through the cinema.

Having established that the basis of Marceau's art is the creation of illusion through a series of conjuring tricks, and that he is the master magician, it remains to determine what Marceau's developing mime in this direction says about him, and about the future of the genre. One critic believes it reveals that "essentially this discipline is a gimmick."[90] For upon mastering the grammar, anyone can render visible the invisible. Indeed, observation of Marceau's classes reveals this to be true. Marceau demonstrates the movement necessary to produce each illusion. His gestures are mimicked by his students as faithfully as possible until they too achieve the desired effect. The emphasis is thus not on creative movement, but on duplication of the master.

Many of the mimes of this school appear to be imitators of Marceau. But in the end, Marceau's facile wit, unique talent for caricature, and remarkably eloquent body allow his work to remain unsurpassed in this category of movement.

The inability of the new generation of Marceauites to advance mime technique raises an important question about the nature of mime itself: Is there a mimic form other than that of Decroux and Marceau? If there is not, then Barrault's lament over the impasse of modern mime seems to be grounded in fact. But there are those, like Jacques Lecoq, who believe that the art of mime can differ radically in form and content from the Marceau genre. Be this as it may, the cul-de-sac of Marceau's art is apparent. Many of his protégés, however, have become successful in other areas of the theatre.

Upon careful review of his thirty years as a mime, it is clear that Marceau has spent most of them in studied self-duplication—he has found a gimmick that he implements over and over again.

> Marceau has originated much of his work himself, but it remains confined, and the fact is—after you've seen him a few times it's hard to get excited. He even repeated himself last night at the City Center, walking along twice with balloons that lift him skyward.[91]

His creative stasis is so noticeable that Clive Barnes wrote a favorable review in 1975 entitled "Vive Meme Chose," to be translated as "Long Live the Same Thing. In an article written just a few weeks later, he has this to say:

> Watching him at the City Center 55th Street Theatre on his first night a couple of weeks ago, it struck me how comparatively little was different since I first encountered him [Marceau] in a small London theatre years ago. . . .
> In 1952 I wrote: "His program is in two parts. The first is

composed of simple mime studies: brilliant, often unforgett-
able sketches. After the interval he presents his pantomimes
of Bip. Bip is a man, he is Marceau." The same notice could
have been written of Marceau today, more than two decades
later.[92]

Marceau does not deny the self-replicating aspect of his art:

"I cannot go beyond 'The Cage' and 'The Maskmaker,'"
says Marceau. "I can make other Cages, other Maskmakers,
yes! But I cannot go beyond."[93]

But when Marceau stated this, he did not see it as an avowal of
his limitations, but as a statement of the artistic perfection he
believes he has attained. He feels he cannot go beyond these
numbers for they represent to him the acme of mimic art. What
Marceau must realize is that they may represent the pinnacle of
his mimic form, but not necessarily the ultimate end of the
evolution of mime itself.

Marceau appears to be in a dual role. He is both the resurrector of the ancient art of mime and the proclaimer of its limitations. His attempts at theorizing—more sentimental description
than critical analysis—do not minimize his achievements. He
has refined the technique, making it more elliptic, the *raccourcis*
more dazzling. In every way, his movements are those of the
virtuoso: controlled, measured, aesthetic. He has returned
mime to the popular art it has traditionally been through his
appealing use of humor and sentiment. He has awakened
worldwide interest in the mime form. Marcel Marceau has actually defined the idiom for this generation.

6

JACQUES LECOQ
(1921–   )

Jacques Lecoq found his common origin with Decroux, Barrault, and Marceau, in the work of Copeau at the Vieux Colombier. Lecoq's link to this tradition is through Jean Dasté, student and son-in-law of Copeau. (Here we see an indication of the incestuous nature of contemporary French mime.) After the Companie des Quinze, a descendant of the Vieux Colombier, in which Dasté worked with mask expert Suzanne Bing, was disbanded, Dasté performed in Barrault's 1935 production of *Autour d'une mère* and was a member of Barrault's Companie des Grands Augustins for a short period in 1936, during the time when Barrault was most under the influence of Artaud. Although Dasté was inspired by Barrault's imagination and spirit, the two men did not get along well.[1] Dasté and his wife Marie-Hélène Copeau went on to establish their own troupe, which Lecoq joined in 1945. The Dastés tried to keep père Copeau's spirit alive. They were inspired by the Noh, but sought to give a new dynamism to its rather static chorus.[2] Dorcy tells us that Dasté was "haunted by the Commedia dell'Arte"[3] as well. He transmitted these passions, his experiences with Barrault and Artaud, as well as his love of improvisation and plastic expression, to the young Lecoq. It is clear that the period with Dasté served as the departure point for the Lecoq technique.

In 1948, Lecoq was invited to teach movement at the University of Padua Theatre School. This was the start of an eight-year sojourn in Italy, during which he became entrenched in the pedagogy of movement. After his establishment of a school at the Piccolo Téatro in Milan, Lecoq's reputation blossomed. He received invitations from theater companies throughout Italy "to give movement to their productions."[4] This began a period of directing and choreographing with sporadic pantomime performances. Lecoq was so much in demand, that during his eight years in Italy, he was responsible for sixty productions, as well as a television pantomime series.[5]

After his Italian success, Lecoq returned to Paris, where, in 1956, he founded his mime school. He continued to direct and make television appearances in France. Lecoq became more and more fascinated by the origins of the various pantomime traditions. In Italy, at the Piccolo, he had continued the exploration of the Commedia he began with Dasté. He examined the ancient mime traditions—the Greek chorus, the acrobatic Roman mime. He was searching for the roots of movement in the theater. Eventually, his school became the center for this work.

Lecoq's mime theory is beat understood if we examine first the classic definition: "The word mime comes from μιμέισθαι (to imitate)."[6] This definition is evidenced in the word "mimicry." Aristotle claims:

Imitation is natural to man from childhood; he differs from other animals in that he is the most imitative. The first things he learns come to him through imitation. Then too all men take pleasure in imitative representations. . . . The reason is that learning things is most enjoyable.[7]

Thus, for Aristotle, miming is part of the learning process. Lecoq explains: "We gain knowledge of things that move through the ability that man has 'to mime' that is, his ability to identify with the world through its reenactment."[8] According to Aristotle and Lecoq then, imitation, or miming, is the source of all learning, as in replicating our sense impressions we gain understanding.

The fire which I see can flame in me. I can know that fire only when I identify with it, and play at being fire. I give my fire to the fire.[9]

This view is supported by anthropologist Marcel Jousse:

Overflowing with a little imitations (mimèmes), the anthropos becomes in many ways all things, and this, without a social language. He is the cat catching the mouse, the rider whipping his horse, the locomotive lending its cars, the plane in the sky; he is always an agent acting out an act. He will play at everything with anything, or better still, at everything without anything.[10]

In observing children it soon becomes clear that they gather knowledge through imitation of animals, adults, toys, etc. For "man knows only what he receives and plays back. It is the gestural playback mechanism of knowledge."[11] Further testimony to this effect is given by anthropologist Alison Jolly:

The child himself analyzes the world into its attributes, and constructs from them objects and organizations of objects. The analysis stems in part from physical action, and much of the child's thought can be considered as "internalized actions."[12]

Lecoq's school is based on the concept of knowledge accrued through movement. He attempts to return the mime to the precognitive state, freeing him to gather a new set of sensory impressions in a neutralized state of naiveté. This requires erasure of past knowledge, which is now tied to the actor's socialized emotional structure, rendering him too socially conditioned to accurately perceive his environment. Lecoq summarizes:

In the beginning, it is necessary to demystify all that we know in order to put ourselves in a state of non-knowing, a state of openness and availability for the rediscovery of the elemental. For now, we no longer see what surrounds us.[13]

To this end, Lecoq has developed an elaborate system of exercises, which will be examined.

If, in his natural state, man identifies with the world through his sense impressions, then "corporal impression is more important than corporal expression."[14]

Implicit in this theory is the idea that thought occurs after movement. The body's impressions and imitations give way to thought. This concept is the source of many difficulties for Lecoq's students, for the natural tendency in adults is to let thought intercede prior to the body's replication of nature, thereby deforming natural movement with socially and intellectually conditioned action.

At this point, a major schism between Decroux and Lecoq becomes apparent. While the latter seeks the unpremeditated, socially uncontaminated natural gesture, Decroux believes:

> Everything is permitted in art, provided it is done on purpose. And since in our art [mime], the body of man is the basic material, the body must imitate thought.[15]

Thus, for Lecoq, the body imitates matter, producing thought, whereas, for Decroux, the body is the very matter which imitates throught. This is the dichotomy between the *mime naturel* of Lecoq, and the *mime statuaire* of Decroux. Lecoq differentiates between these two as the *mime de fond* (translated as "fundamental", "basic," "heart," "root," or "essence" mime"), which he calls "mime," versus the *mime de forme* (translated as "form", "shape" or "mannered" mime), which he calls "pantomime." Lecoq believes that the *mime de fond* must be the basis for all movement:

> It is in the gesture under the gesture, in the gesture behind the word, in the movement of matter, sounds, colors and lights that the school finds its basis.[16]

To further differentiate between the *mime de forme* (pantomime) and the *mime de fond* (mime), they must be analyzed as communication systems, in that they both serve as means of transmitting complex messages. This anthropological view of language supports Lecoq's concept of two gesture systems:

> Wherever gesture systems occur, they appear to develop by reasons of linguistic diversity, that is, to supply a rough means of communication between peoples who speak mutually unintelligible tongues. If this is true, then modern gesture systems are no relic of an early and primitive form of symbolizing; they are merely secondary systems to be used when, and only when, the infinitely superior means of communication by oral symbols fails.[17]

The secondary communication system corresponds to the *pantomime blanche* of Deburau, and although radically different in style, to the pantomime of Decroux and Marceau, which shares their highly developed aesthetics. Lecoq wants to recapture the "primitive form of symbolizing" that existed before the development of a sophisticated oral tradition, as this would be a more immediate and direct form of expression. He wants the *mime de fond* to be a primary gesture system. It follows that there are two types of silence corresponding to the two mimes:

> The *silence de fond* where the word does not yet exist, is a necessity, and the gesture is pure versus the superficial and mutilated silence, where gesture imitates, and tries in vain to replace the word, which has already said everything.[18]

If gesture exists before thought, then it must also exist before the word, as language is predicated on thought. Therefore Lecoq refuses all grammatical analogies, which he believes orient mime away from its origins.

If we analyze the development of man, it is clear that movement precedes language in the individual and in the anthropological sense as well.[19] The goal of Lecoq is to send his students back to the level of cognition and gesture preceding the word.

> The goal therefore, is not to replace words with gestures, (pantomime), but to find the gesture of the word, the actions for the verbs in the profound silence in which they were born.[20]

Gesture precedes knowledge.
Gesture precedes thought.
Gesture precedes language.
Lecoq believes that voice as a communication system exists on two levels, similar to the dual gesture languages: There is a primitive sound that exists prior to formal language, but that expresses primal needs; i.e., the scream, the groan, the cry, and there is the developed formal phonal pattern of language. Paralleling his approach to movement, Lecoq wants the mime to use only those sounds that are part of a primary communication system. Voice is analagous to gesture in that imitating sounds also yields knowledge. Therefore, as the mime must rediscover his environment through imitative action, he must also learn through imitative sound. As only primal sounds should be coupled with mime, Lecoq believes the human voice

should only be heard when the actor is pushed to the precipice between *"le cri ou le crève"* (the scream or death).[21] This is the point at which physical need demands sound. This is more emotionally immediate than developed language. Here Lecoq's theories echo Artaud.

Lecoq, unlike Decroux and Marceau, is not opposed to language being integrated with mime, provided that the sounds have been produced as the results of physical needs:

> A word should be charged with corporal impression; the definition in itself is not enough.
> In white pantomime, gesture defines the word.[22]

This integration of language and mime enlarges the scope of creative possibilities available to the Lecoq disciple, who is not limited by the concept of gesture functioning only in silence. Lecoq believes that mime, like all art forms should entail a constant search for new forms of expression, and should have no imposed boundaries.[23]

This is the progression of Lecoq's theories:

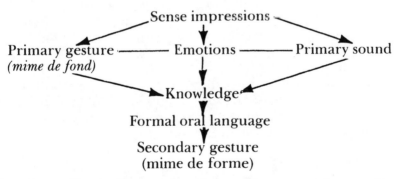

Then, according to Lecoq, sense impressions precede conscious recognition of emotion. Hence, Lecoq claims his system is "the opposite of the Method,"[24] the Stanislavski system, which presupposes intellectual justification for feeling or inner need. The "objective" or recognized emotional need, in the Stanislavski sense, precedes the action, it determines the action. Lecoq feels that sense impression determines the emotion and the action, and has developed a series of exercises that demonstrate this principle.

In summary, the *mime de forme*, dependent upon sophisticated linguistic analogies, can occur only after primitive mime (the *mime de fond*), that is, after an oral language has been formalized in a more advanced culture or society, for ". . . culture came into being only when man learned to symbolize."[25] Since the two gesture systems occur at different points in time, Lecoq refers to them as the *mime du début* (mime of the beginning or *mime de fond*), and as the *mime de la fin* (mime of the end or *mime de forme*). A similar categorization of human gesture patterns as seen in relation to culture has been formulated by Alison Jolly:

> Although "pure intention movements," autonomic expressions, and so forth may communicate emotion, we do not call them displays until they have reached the second stage, that of ritualization. Ritualization, in the biological sense, means that an item of behavior has been subject to selection that has increased its communicative value—in particular that has made it less ambiguous, more easily interpreted.
>
> Ritualized behavior can be recognized by the properties that resemble human ritual. First, it is exaggerated. . . . Second it is stereotyped, stylized. A gesture is less ambiguous if it is always performed in a single form.[26]

If mime exists when man is in a brute, nonacculturated state, then pantomime, in its "stereotyped, stylized" form, exists in a state of advanced socialization, or ritualization. This further explains Lecoq's concept of *mime du début* (mime) versus *mime de la fin* (pantomime).

Jolly claims that later languages are more readily understood. The semiologist Georges Mounin explains the difference in intelligibility through a linguistic examination of levels of meaning in mime and pantomime:

> The clear separation occurs between denotative and connotative meaning. Pantomime licensed and sought after the totally social and totally transparent gesture, which in its value as gesture would be common to all members of the same socio-cultural community. It is the "gestural stereotype," common to all, in brief, a denotation in the sense which linguists use this term. One senses, on the contrary, with contemporary mime, a privileged search for everything which a gesture common to all can "evoke, suggest, excite or imply in a clear or vague manner," and this is strictly, if not inevitably, individual—in brief, the connotation of gesture in the sense which linguists use this term.[27]

Thus, pantomime is denotative because it relies on the preexistent language, whereas, mime is connotative since it should seek to emulate the gestural expression prior to language, where lacking any definitional system, all gesture was connotative in meaning.

It is interesting to contrast the socioculturally limited stereotypes of the old pantomime to Jung's concept of archetypes that transcend all cultures.[28] Jung believes that there is material in the subconscious of man that links him to other men regardless of time or culture; that the subconscious symbols would precede culture and be common to all, regardless of social context. These symbols would be connotative in structure.

Lecoq then, is searching for archetypical movement and culturally transcendental meanings that could depend on both the conscious and the subconscious for interpretation. Therefore the subconscious connotation would be as significant as the conscious, social, denotative meaning.

Lecoq's mime need have no relation to realism—*realism* in the sense that Marceau uses the term: allusion to, or illusion of the easily recognized objects of reality. Therefore, although Lecoq defines mime as the imitation of nature, he does not seek the codified illusion of reality. What is sought instead is the gestural rendering of the essence of reality, a reality that may be beyond the tangible. The essential is not intellectually deduced but primally experienced. The sensory reeducation of the mime enables him to discover the gestural archetype.

> Anyone can imitate life without being able to act on the stage.
> The difference comes from what the talented, skilled, and trained actor extracts consciously and intuitively from what he observes—a common point of gesture among all men, a sort of common denominator.[29]

Mounin explains the differences in the two approaches to mime:

> All that we know about pantomime suggests that it tended towards, and still tends towards the constitution of an analogous code where the gesture of reality is symbolized by the theatrical gesture. . . . It is obvious that modern mime is characterized by an attempt to preserve from the code only

the minimum necessary to insure intelligibility . . . modern mime can transmit nonsocialized experiences, personal, indecipherable messages only through violation of the code without destroying it, in order to safeguard an important transmissibility.[30]

The code is no longer the only essential vehicle for the message. Decroux would have some difficulty with this concept. He claims:

Since form dictates function, since the human form is unchangeable, since the body of man is condemned to resemble the body of man, meaning is determined despite him.[31]

The Mummenschanz, a company of young Lecoq disciples, has shown that man can renounce the human identity, creating abstract forms that serve to mask not only the face but the human body as well. Often "their masked figures are . . . of fantasy shapes of no identifiable form."[32] Mime of this nature can be totally nonrepresentational.

Lecoq believes it is through such an approach to mime that it can, as an art form, be part of the twentieth century.

The great artists of this century have sought to give visible form to the "life behind things" and so their works are a symbolic expression of a world behind consciousness.[33]

Therefore, mime, when unfettered to denotative social meaning, can enter the realm of modern abstract art, where

nothing in works of non-figurative art reminds the spectator of his own world . . . and yet, without any question, there is a human bond.[34]

Abstract and *symbolic* mean something very different to Lecoq than they did to Decroux. As these concepts have changed in the plastic arts since the late 1920s when Decroux was first formulating his theories, so they were to change in their application to corporal expression twenty-five years later when Lecoq was developing his concept of mime. Lecoq's mime may therefore have no relationship to tangible reality, and be evocative only of inner states of consciousness, whereas *abstract* to Decroux initially meant abstraction of the physically real though in later years, he sought more abstract forms of expression as well.

Lecoq believes that an analysis of theater history reveals a cyclical development of style. When a particular form reaches its full development, it becomes overused until it disintegrates into a cliché. This is followed by a period of creative searching for new forms. Mime has a particular role in this process. Lecoq believes:

> In the history of the theatre, mime as an isolated art form has no permanence. It appears in certain particular eras: at the end of one theatre or at the beginning of another. It sustains action and conserves gesture during the limited time period, where the theatre having lost the force of words, renews its forms.[35]

Hence, he claims that upon examining the history of mime, it is clearly resuscitated in periods of decadence; i.e., Greece and Rome.[36] This is because during periods of decadence, humans must return to their roots, redefine their values, justify anew their existence. They therefore seek within their bare physical being for new meanings. We are presently in such an era, but Lecoq believes his school must not function for today, but for the great theatrical era towards which we are building.[37]

In this historical perspective, the *mime de la fin* (pantomime) occurs at the end of an era in the theater in which form is well defined. The *mime du début* (mime) occurs when the theater is seeking redefinition.

The *mime du début* works toward the new theater that will grow out of the remains of the old style, and therefore is predicated on a search for new meanings. Lecoq's school works toward the future, the mime of a great epoch in the theater, in which he foresees the projection of mime toward dance and theater.[38] This would be a move toward symbolic gesture in the Jungian sense. It is in opposition to the dependence on cliché exemplified by the old pantomime.

Lecoq is against the *mime de la fin,* because he believes it to be based on a meaningless demonstration of technical virtuosity inspired by superficial aestheticism:

> He is opposed to stereotyped gesture, "artistic and conventional gesture of another era, narcissistic gesture, a gesture

just for the sake of itself, the pretentious beautiful gesture, gestural aestheticism." On the contrary, the mime's style should be "a distillation of gesture towards a solitary symbol of all gesture."[39]

He further explains:

Mime evolves in silence, there where the word is not yet permitted, or no longer permitted. If I push gesture too far, I can no longer speak: gesture engages action in silence. When gesture replaces the word, that is called pantomime; such was the case with Roman pantomime and with the white pantomime (Pierrot).

During the Roman era, one mimed philosophical discourses, and one day, the great mime Roscius mimed a discourse of Cicero with his feet; this marked the end of pantomime, which was killed by its own virtuosity.[40]

In protest against the virtuoso performance, Lecoq even goes as far as to say: "If a mime is to be interesting, he should mime badly."[41]

"We address ourselves to the student as a creative being, and not as an interpreter of a proposed aesthetic," says Lecoq.[42] Believing this, he is opposed to the idea of codification, which, for him, violates the whole premise of an art form, as it produces a fixed aesthetics that turns the artist into an interpreter, not a creator. The codification forces our criteria for artistic judgment to be the technical virtuosity of the artist in his interpretation of a fixed form. It imposes limits on creativity, resulting in the inevitable cliché. Under the code, we are not interested in the discovery of new styles, but in the stylization of old forms.

Lecoq's mime depends on the "refutation of the recipe."[43] He warns his students to "avoid the temptation toward the absolute."[44] He is philosophically opposed to the imposition of the Decroux *grammaire* and claims, "Definitions kill mime. . . . I am against Marceau's locking shut the development of mime."[45] Lecoq is firmly "against the idea of limitations" being placed on an art form.[46] Marceau has stated that he cannot go beyond his present mime.[47] It is this sense of a limit being placed on artistic creation that leads Lecoq to state: "The Marceauites have killed mime."[48]

It is clear that Lecoq's concepts differ radically from the self-conscious aesthetics of Decroux and the stylized virtuosity of Marcel Marceau.

The implementation of Lecoq's philosophy is effected by an elaborate system of exercises designed to lead the actor to the *mime de fond*. Lecoq gives a general overview of his technique:

> I begin with the process of forgetting. Then demystification. We return to zero through masks and decontraction. We begin again to gather knowledge through the body. When we have recognized the world through the body, we can express ourselves.
>
> Next we attempt new experiences—expressive masks, the Commedia, etc.
>
> After experimenting with these different means of expression, one must choose the place where he is happiest.
>
> Last, one adds the level of symbolism to the montage. One attempts a level of acting which goes toward the symbol.[49]

Each step in this process corresponds to a particular type of mask, which, when combined with improvisation, enables the mime to achieve these goals. Thus Lecoq continues the masked improvisational approach to corporal training begun by Copeau and Suzanne Bing, and sustained by Dasté and Decroux.

Lecoq sees the mask as a multifaceted tool:

> They [masks] facilitate the discovery of the central point, the essence of a relationship, or a conflict, the discovery of the gesture which is the sum of all gestures, the word which represents all words.[50]

Lecoq uses five basic types of masks: neutral, expressive, larval, Commedia, and red clown's nose. Each has a function that will be examined in context.

First, an analysis of the "forgetting process:"

> The first year is a year of demystification of ready-made ideas. It creates a state of readiness and availability of the physical and mental sensibilities of the student. There is a recognition of life as it is, through observation of the everyday occurrence. We do not speak of theatre but of life.[51]

Lecoq erases the past through the neutral mask. This expressionless, nonpsychological mask creates a barrier between the student and his inner self. "Neutral," Lecoq explains, "does not mean absent. It means without a past, open, ready. One cannot act psychologically because the eye doesn't travel. The eye is replaced by the head."[52] As the eye represents the inner man, the neutral mask deflects the emphasis from the eye which is only barely visible, and places it instead on the movement of the head which is more generalized and less psychologically oriented. The audience perceives the movement of the head and not the eye. If the eradication of an actor's emotional past were all the neutral mask accomplished, Lecoq and Decroux would be implementing this mask in identical fashion. But Lecoq believes the mask can do more than facilitate the performance of, in Decroux's words, "contradictory things without seeming ridiculous."[53] Lecoq takes the power of the neutral mask a step further. He sees its erasure of the Self as a liberation that permits the mime to rediscover the world in a newly attained state of nonknowing. The dichotomy between the two men is apparent: this application of the neutral mask is antithetical to Decroux's *mime statuaire,* which relies upon intellectual cognition; at the same time, it is crucial to Lecoq'e *mime naturel* which is based on the mime's sensory reeducation.

Through the neutral mask, Lecoq is trying to return his student to the precognitive state, where he is free to gather fresh mimic impressions.

> The individual becomes a blank page. He holds no opinion and has no inner searching. Everything is erased so he can start from scratch, seeing things for the first time. This corresponds to a state of total relaxation.[54]

With his face covered, and words forbidden, the student must live through his body.

Lecoq sees two approaches to the neutral mask:

> In approaching the neutral mask there are two possible roads:
> 1. Improvisation starting with the interior state towards the exterior.
> 2. The purely technical analysis of the human body and everything that moves.
> The second approach is the more solid one, and more faithful to the Aristotelian concept of mime—to try to figure out scientifically how something moves.

The basis of the netural mask is to attain a state of stability without conflicts.

It is the mask of calm.

One can never be sick under the neutral mask.

It is the discovery of the self, but not through the self.[55]

Under the neutral mask, Lecoq sends his students through a series of exercises designed to aid the rediscovery of the world around them. Many of these are based on the original exercises developed by Jacques Copeau and Suzanne Bing at the Vieux Colombier.

Identification aux matières (Identification with Matter): This exercise is the first step in the gathering of knowledge through the body. The goal is for the mime to come to a deeper understanding of the world around him through a physical identification with the essential qualities of various materials. It evolves into increasingly more complicated exercises.

Starting from a state of masked neutrality (relaxed and open), the actor must identify with and incarnate some material: e.g., steel, fire, ice. In order to accomplish this, the mime must first acknowledge that all matter moves. He must find the inner rhythm of that material, and translate it into his respiration, allowing for all the properties of the chosen material.

When the actor has succeeded in identifying with different elements, he is ready to take the exercise a step further. Now he must, in addition to movement and respiration, add sound— the essential sound of his chosen element, or in Lecoq's words, the actor must "find the place where gesture meets sound."[56]

When the mime is proficient in this identification process, and has deepened his knowledge of the inner life of things through mimesis, the exercise is enlarged to *Le Choeur des Matières* (The chorus of matter). This is a prelude to the more advanced choral work.

The performers are divided into groups. Each group represents a specific material. Now the actor must be sensitive not only to the inner rhythm of matter, but to the rhythm and respiration of his fellow students. They must blend with their element and with each other, living together as molecules of the element. Then, as before, the dimension of sound is added.

The next step is *La rencontre des matières* (The meeting of matter). Each elemental chorus encounters another, reacting according to the properties of their respective materials, sens-

ing the essential qualities of the matter represented by its opposing group: e.g., fire should melt ice, gum should stick to
steel.

Now the actor has passed through demystification and the
regathering of knowledge. He is ready to attempt a higher
theatrical level.

The mimes are told to play characters whose personalities
correspond to certain materials. They interact as human beings
who are like ice, steel, air, etc. The goal is to discover the emotional state that corresponds to the essence of the elements.

The development of this exercise leads the actor to character,
while deepening his perceptions of the environment in which
he lives. Character is arrived at through physical impression, in
keeping with the Lecoq philosophy.

Identifying the correct rhythm of matter, translating it into
respiration, then recognizing the emotional state provoked by
this rhythm is the essential component of these exercises. The
concept of respiration inducing emotion is that of Artaud's
Kabbale, which Lecoq adapts to his own needs. It is further
expanded to include identification with animals, sounds, light,
and so on. Lecoq summarizes:

> We play people, elements, animals, plants, trees, colors,
> lights, matter, sounds—going beyond their images, gaining
> knowledge of their space, their rhythm, their breath through
> improvisation.[57]

The work with the neutral mask is brought to the Greek
chorus, which Lecoq believes to be the embodiment of neutrality as "it is all-knowing."[58] Since its thrust is exterior, it is
therefore nonpsychological. To establish this external focus,
Lecoq has developed the exercise, *Equilibre du plateau* (Balance
of the stage).

There is an intangible balance between the hero and the
chorus. His emotional weight equals that of the entire chorus.
As he moves about the stage, the chorus must regroup itself in
order to maintain the psychological equilibrium of the playing
space. This balance is maintained only through each individual's focusing on the hero, and relating to each other only
through his movements. "The chorus is together without looking at each other because they are looking at the same thing."[59]
This exercise becomes more than a mere geometric apportion-

ment of people. In fact, Lecoq warns against falling prey to the temptation toward geometric positioning. With sensitive actors, this exercise itself becomes a drama, for, as Lecoq reminds us: "the mere presence of man in space is dramatic."[60] As such, this exercise raises the level of action toward the symbol, the ultimate goal for Lecoq.

Lecoq believes it is important for the mime to discover movement in total economy, that is, the least amount of movement and energy needed to accomplish an action. The economical gesture is a primary building block in the Lecoq technique. He sees all style as the selective enlargement or distortion of the neutral and economical. The mime must understand the concept of the essential before he can go beyond it. His sensory reeducation enables him to pare down gesture to its minimal components.

> The analysis of the movements of physical actions in total economy (the least effort for the maximum result), and the neutral state, allow us to understand the manifestations of life in a state of perpetual discovery. . . .[61]

In order for them to discover neutrality in total economy of physical energy, Lecoq has his students analyze a series of simple movement studies. Let us say a bartender is making a cocktail. The actor must determine the exact series of movements necessary to complete the act. This must be broken down into separate attitudes, with a pause between each one. The simple act of mixing a drink may be broken down into as many as two hundred separate components. These must be pared away until only the essential movements remain. They should be neutral and contain no emotional message. When these units have been established, the actor must find the sound that correponds to each action. In this manner, the actor learns how to perform pure nonpsychological movements; he learns to be expressive in silence, without creating a parody of everyday life.

When the neutral and economical gesture has been attained, the mime is ready to add stylization. Stylization, then, is the manner in which the economical and neutral gesture is altered. For example, Lecoq believes that the comic effect occurs when one follows through to the succeeding actions before realizing that an error has been made; i.e., a rower is rowing a boat; if the mime has examined this movement in economy, he knows the necessary series of attitudes to execute this action. If the rower loses his oar, in order to achieve the comic effect, he must not realize the loss until two or three attitudes later, at which point he reacts with surprise. The longer it takes to realize the error (time is measured by the number of successive attitudes that have transpired), the denser the character is.[62] This, for Lecoq, is the essence of comic movement.

After the neutral, economical gesture is established, Lecoq has his students improvise with various types of masks that permit stylization.

The *masque expressif* represents a fixed psychological character: e.g., the idiot, the haughty, the old man, the beauty. If worn properly, the fixed face should force the body, and then the emotions, to follow. Lecoq believes that there is a dialogue between the mask and its wearer, that the mask draws something out of the actor.[63] The greater the rapport between mask and wearer, the greater the dimension of meaning.

When the mime has learned to recognize the mask and let it guide him, Lecoq introduces the *contre-masque*. Here, the actor must play the opposite of the character indicated by the external mask:

> To play the ultra-intellectual under the mask of the idiot. Youth under the mask of age. Humility under the mask of pride.
> Then, the character is no longer a half-alive caricature, but a character who bears an internal conflict. Man is in conflict with himself. It is already a drama, without need of a dramatic situation.[64]

These exercises grow into multi-character improvisations. The level of action is raised to realism, and then beyond realism, for everything is larger than life under the mask. Once again, Lecoq is moving toward the symbol.

Next Lecoq uses abstract larval masks as a stimulus for the imagination. These masks are of sculpted, large, white, bizarre, abstract forms. They are nonhuman, and yet, they evoke a human quality. Each mask creates an emotional state. The mime must explore the expressive possibilities of these haunting masks. The Mummenschanz have used Lecoq's exercises with these particular masks to develop a gamut of images, ranging from animal incarnations to phantoms of the subconscious.

This mask work is based on the concept of the external physical manifestation acting upon the psyche to create an internal state. This is clearly in opposition to the Method school. Other exercises also reflect this approach.

Believing that the physical senses evoke an emotional state, Lecoq has his students isolate various parts of the body and position them differently, noting that as one angles the head or the pelvis, a change in emotional state accompanies the shift. Through this procedure, the student explores the relationship between the physical and the emotional.

In the same vein, Lecoq has developed exercises in which the actor must imagine a change in his physical environment and relate this to his emotional disposition. In one such exercise, *Le voyage*, he has the actor walk through a variety of imaginary terrains, always altering his interior state in relation to the external environment. The difficulty for the student is in letting the change happen viscerally without playing the feeling artificially.

Furthering the concept of the physical evoking the emotional, Lecoq has developed a variety of scales. The following exercises require that the mime hold an emotional level without going beyond it, while being sensitive to the emotional state of those with whom he shares the stage. Each actor must intensify the emotional level established by the preceding actor to enter the stage. When the actor entering the stage raises the level, all those present on the stage must raise their feelings to meet the newly established intensity of feeling. In the *Gamme de peur* (scale of fear), we move from neutrality of the first actor through the barely perceivable anxiety of the second, up the scale to fear, terror, and death. In the *Gamme de rire*, (scale of laughter), we move from neutrality, to the smirk, smile, giggle, laughter, hysterics. Once again, each actor must raise the preceding level, while all the others must sense his emotions and intensify theirs accordingly.

Lecoq reminds his students that the Commedia is always played at the highest level of intensity—beyond the laugh, beyond terror.

Lecoq stresses the importance of respiration for the mime. He has a repertoire of improvisations in which the actor learns that breath is the key to the emotions and to the message: e.g., in the chase, as the actor flees an imaginary pursuer, he hides in a doorway. If he inhales at this point, the audience will perceive that he is still in danger, for inhalation creates contraction and tension. If he exhales, the physical message will be that he is safe, for with exhalation there is an accompanying relaxation. Breath can create conflict between the gesture and the emotions, says Lecoq.[65] He challenges his students to create great passion while holding their breath. The vital nature of respiration is clear.

These exercises bring the actor to the Commedia dell'Arte, which Lecoq sees as "an enlargement of the essential,"[66] for in the Commedia, "all passions are pushed to an extreme, and the question is not that of life but of survival."[67]

The Commedia work is of great importance to Lecoq. Language enters his work here, and it marks the point where "the scream seeks the sign."[68] Here certain stereotyped gesture is representative of each masked character. The burden for the actor, in this case, is to play the stereotype, letting fixed external movements and the mask create the internal character.

The Commedia's exaggerated style permits the implementation of all Lecoq's concepts and techniques:

1. Rapport between the actor and the mask.
2. Gesture begetting character.
3. Movement for survival, not for superficial aesthetics.
4. Word meeting gesture.
5. Improvisation through the *lazzi.*
6. External and internal rhythm.
7. Character relationships.
8. Play of attitudes.
9. The gesture that is the sum of all gesture.
10. The word that is the sum of all words.

The last and all-important step in the Lecoq training is the discovery of one's clown. It is significant work, for here the mime finally situates himself in relation to the modern world. Once again the mask is used, this time, the smallest mask of all, the red clown's nose. The mime is more naked than ever before.

The individual's clown is the repressed self, repressed because its expression would entail socially unacceptable behavior.

It deals with bringing out of each individual the child which has grown up inside of him, and which society does not permit him to express. The inner child has become for many of us a source of shame. This buried being made of solitude, missed experiences and hidden faults belongs to us.[69]

This theory is reiterated by the Polish philosopher Kolakowski:

> The clown is he who, although moving in high society, is not a part of it, and tells unpleasant things to everybody in it; he, who disputes everything regarded as evident. He would not be able to do this, if he were part of that society himself; then he could at most be a drawing-room scandal-monger. The Clown must stand aside and observe good society from the outside. . . . The philosophy of Clowns is the philosophy that in every epoch shows up as doubtful what has been regarded as most certain. . . .[70]

Exposing one's clown is often a very painful process for the actor. It means confronting the aspects of the personality one prefers to deny.

> To express one's clown, that means to come face to face with one's Self, yet still stand outside one's Self, at the small distance where humor is located. It is an indispensable dimension in the search for knowledge.[71]

In Lecoq's early exercises he wants to aid the actor in acquiring knowledge of the world around him, but with the clown, he is leading the actor to the knowledge most difficult to attain—knowledge of oneself.

As the repressed self is linked to current social standards of comportment, so the material of the clown is intrinsically linked to the society of its times. Therefore, the clown metamorphoses as society evolves.

The clowns of the early part of this century—Chaplin, Keaton, Lloyd—dealt with the problems of man versus the machine, man and modernization, the desperate attempt to maintain humanity in an age that worships technology. But today, we are all children of these "modern times." The clown's material lies elsewhere if he is to be truly reflective of society's most sensitive issues. We have moved from fear of the machine to fear of becoming no more than a mere cog in that machine. Henri Bergson notes:

> The attitudes, gestures and movements of the human body
> are laughable in exact proportion as that body reminds us of
> a mere machine.[72]

Today's clown reflects this paranoia of technology, and uses it as
a source of humor.

Lecoq believes that "only in great freedom can the individual
be himself and only himself. It is the experience of solitude."[73]
This idea links the clown to existential theory. The expression
of the inner self isolates and alienates man from society, but it is
the only way to be truly free. "Self humour," says Lecoq, "is the
only true alienation effect."[74]

Lecoq believes that Beckett is the greatest author of modern
mime, because he understands the true nature of the clown.[75]
Jean Anouilh echoes this thought, describing *Waiting for Godot*
as "a music hall sketch of Pascal's *Pensées* performed by the
Fratellini clowns."[76] ". . . the improvisations of the two tramps
suggest that the endless semantic speculations and misunder-
standings of the Commedia dell'Arte," says Beckett critic
Michael Robinson.[77] Thus Lecoq sees the clown as the manifestation of the absurdity of our existence. It represents the
ultimate irony in that freedom begets alienation; yet he feels it
is imperative that the actor discover his clown, for he believes
the clown to be the only hero of our times.

The theory and technique of Jacques Lecoq are based on the
central idea of creative freedom. He liberates the mime from
his past, from preconceived notions of the world and his relation to it, subjecting him to a sensory rediscovery of his environment and his hidden inner Self. He imposes no system, no
ready-made aesthetics. Those who have worked with Lecoq
choose varied and divergent paths. Some return to the traditional theater, bringing to the text the vigor of movement.
Others, such as Rufus and Pierre Byland, have continued the
exploration of the clown. The Mummenschanz seek the expressive possibilities of the mask and the phantoms of the subconscious. These divergences are the goal of the Lecoq system. He
believes the ultimate end of his training should be

> to liberate mime from the sclerosis of formalisms, creating
> the fundamentals of a dramatic formation completely based
> on the body, pitting the student face to face with himself in a
> state of perpetual discovery.[78]

Many protégés of Decroux and Marceau do not consider the work of Jacques Lecoq as fundamental to the mime renaissance. They claim his work to be a distinct discipline that followed the work of Messieurs Decroux, Barrault, and Marceau chronologically, but that has no other tie to the earlier theories. But the genealogy offered in the introductory chapter clearly traces Lecoq's roots back to Jacques Copeau—the common source of all this book's subjects. Further, where Lecoq departs from the schools of Decroux and Marceau, he does so as a conscious rebellion. Lecoq has initiated a countermovement that remains part of the modern French mime form. Although the impact of Jacques Lecoq's theories and training is yet to be realized, there is a major new movement afoot, and it cannot be ignored.

7

CONCLUSION

Having analyzed the work of the four major French mimes of the twentieth century, there remains one question to be answered: Is there a unique genre that is "modern French mime," or are these four men isolated phenomena? Although each man has developed his individual style, aesthetic, and perspective on the art, there are two factors that unite them and underscore their common origins.

First, modern French mime differs from the ancient tradition of mime and pantomime in its conscious formal aesthetics, its need to establish itself as a viable art form, and in the cerebral approach to movement that all four men insist upon as a prerequisite for action.

Second, although mime and pantomime have been primarily corporal arts, never before has mime so violently and consciously repudiated the word, reviled the cliché, and waged war against denotative meaning. In the silent pantomime of the eighteenth and nineteenth centuries, the mime style sought to replace the word suppressed by law. When the ban was lifted, Pierrot was drowned in the deluge of words that followed. Therefore, Barrault calls the old pantomime form a mute art, implying the muzzled word, as opposed to the elected silent art of the modern era. Although Barrault and Lecoq permit sounds and words with mime, they do so with the clear understanding that the word exists only as a connotative symbol or as the essential synthesis of all words.

The silence of modern French mime began as a rebellion against the literary French culture:

Before any poetic event can happen the cultural clatter must be stopped.

The silence of the French poet arises on the opposite side of the globe from the silence of the Kansas farmhand.

With the latter silence just is, an emptiness coming from American space and time.

The Frenchman has to will his silence, he struggles for it, in it he purifies himself of the past, makes himself ready. . . .[1]

Relating to this need, all four men claim their mime is born in silence. For Decroux, mime is born in the silence that denies the tyranny of the word and the incessant rhetoric of the French theatrical tradition. For Barrault, mime is born in the silence that expresses the solitude of existence, the silence of a mystic presence. Marceau's mime is born in the silence that sustains illusion. And Lecoq believes mime is born in the silence of primitive man before the discovery of the word and the language that would eventually imprison the expressive range of the body.

This self-conscious theorizing, this rejection of literal meanings and the literary culture, these two attributes establish modern French mime as a distinctly new phenomenon. They are not haphazard qualities; they relate contemporary mime to the major thrust of modern art.

Clarifying the relationship between the new mime and modern aesthetic thought requires an identification of "the Paris style" or "Paris Modern"[2]—critic Harold Rosenberg's labels for that unique synthesis of contemporary science, psychology, politics, and art that was the hallmark of that city during the first half of this century: "Paris has been synonymous with Modernism in the sense of the special style and tempo of our consciousness."[3] As the new mime was born in the Paris of that era, it is imperative that the essential qualities of "the Paris style" be explicated: in order to correlate the divergent styles of the four mimes analyzed in this work with the Paris Modern, it should be emphasized that the Paris style is not a fixed form, but an ever-evolving composite of confluent trends, reflecting multiple influences. The only constants are conscious aesthetic theorizing coupled with a search for new forms, and the consistent repudiation of naturalism, with its literal replication of reality.

The first movement to be considered a precursor of Paris Modern is symbolism. Its concept of a psychic reality beyond the tangible, of connotative meanings to be deciphered apart from denotative plot lines, of sensory bombardment for effect, appears now as a signpost for twentieth-century aesthetic thought. Despite its emphasis away from literal meanings, symbolism began as a movement in poetry, an art dependent upon the word, but it attempted to organize language in such a way as to facilitate connotative interpretation, by creating the aura of the magic world of the daydream, of revery unfettered to the organized structure of reality. When symbolism was applied to the theater, the search beyond the literal gave way to the idea that silence can often communicate more than the word. The presence of silence dominates the literary French theater for the first time, directly linking this movement to modern mime. Decroux's work is distinctly related to the symbolist concept of connotative meaning. Further, Artaud's experiences with the late symbolist theater provide a direct bloodline from symbolism to modern mime.

Similar probings beyond naturalism were evident in the visual arts. Painting turned to impressionism, the creation of the illusion of the real that means more than the real, and later to cubism with its concern for total effect rather than the representation of reality.

In 1899, with the publication of Freud's *Interpretation of Dreams,* came the awareness of an even deeper psychic reality—the world of the subconscious and its symbols. The French were quick to assimilate the implications of this world of the psyche. Surrealism vividly portrayed the workings of the subconscious, concretizing its symbols.

As the depths of the human mind were explored, art began to depict man's hallucinations and dreams. Psychological realism was expanded into expressionism—the portrayal of a world filtered through the emotions. Theater became the site of the exteriorization of man's animal drives, an echo chamber for the primal scream.

Eventually, the workings of the inner mind were expressed in total abstraction. Less and less of tangible reality was present in art. Paris Modern culminated in the depiction of hieroglyphs of the subconscious, in the portrayal of abstract psychological archetypes, in the suggestion of meaning through totally nonrepresentational forms.

This rejection of literal meaning is exemplified by the work of Paris Modern's paramount literary figure—James Joyce. His career spans the entire era of Paris Modern, and his work reflects the evolution of the Paris aesthetics. His early writing expresses the sensory immediacy of the symbolists, an attempt to have each word express more than its mere literal meaning. Freudian psychology moves the work of Joyce's middle years into a stream of consciousness style that uses the word to depict the flow of inner states. The need for Aristotelian plot line diminishes. In *Finnegan's Wake,* literal linear structure is buried under sensory word images and quadralingual puns, building meaning upon meaning until denotations are lost and only the connotative effect of the montage remains. Joyce is the archetype of the Paris style.

Modern mime is a result of the intersection of two lines of force: historical tradition and the new aesthetics. The ban of the spoken word during the late eighteenth and early nineteenth centuries in all but the state theaters united with the constant rebellion against the power of the word in the literary French culture to keep the pantomime form alive in France long after its European decline. This preexistent tradition interacted with what Barrault calls "the golden age of aesthetics" that engendered "the Paris style" to produce the modern mime form.

Jacques Copeau was the catalyst in the creation of this compound form, for it was he who first recognized the possibility of a synthesis of the old tradition with the new aesthetics combining the strengths of both. The new mime, growing out of Copeau's vision, reflects for each mime studied, various doses of the prevalent Paris aesthetic ideology and ancient tradition.

In this context, Decroux's major accomplishment was his persuasive projection of the idea that the human body can also refuse the mere photographic reproduction of naturalistic gesture, and seek instead the essence of gesture, the abstraction of movement.

Although mime and pantomime of past eras have diverse characteristics, there is still one quality that was common to all forms until the twentieth century—the literal quality of gesture. Action on the stage corresponded to the manner of performing that action (or "verb") in life. if the mime wished to give the appearance of walking, he simply walked across the stage the way he would walk down the street. The sense of time and space was established with a change of sets, or enough text to establish the new locale. Such was the case with climbing, lift-

ing, running, etc. Each of these activities was performed natu-
ralistically. To facilitate this real-life mime, props were part of
the performance; minimal as they were, they were there. The
emphasis was still on physical prowess, but other things were
allowed to share the stage: texts, sets, props, music, dance,
song, used in different measure in different periods. In the
nineteenth century, although the mime was silent, it still called
upon the traditional apparatus of the theater.

Decroux, the first man to conceive of modern abstract mime,
freed movement from the vestiges of naturalism by banning all
the traditional elements of the theater of past eras: sets, props,
realistic costumes and text. Only the mask remains for its ability
to abstract the actor's individual identity. With the self-
conscious asesthetics typical of Paris Modern, he codified a
method of creating the illusion of reality without recourse to
any component of that reality and developed a transmissible
technique through which he physicalizes the metaphysical. Decroux is most successful in this. Perhaps his greatest accomplishment is his expansion of the traditional concepts of theatrical gesture through the creation of a vocabulary with which one
can talk about the abstraction of movement in mime.

Although Decroux broke new ground, he did not totally succeed in freeing mime from constraints. He replaced the tyranny of denotative meaning with an obsessive preoccupation
with technique, a preoccupation that was perhaps necessary to
establish the viability of modern mime as an independent art
form.

Decroux is thus clearly related to the early stages of Paris
Modern. He has captured its cerebral search for new forms of
expression. But in terms of the degree of abstraction he has
attained in mime gesture, he is fundamentally working in the
framework of the impressionists and cubists, who view their art
as the refraction of reality, and use the term *abstract* to mean the
expression of the essential properties of reality. Although Decroux saw modern mime as a "system of unconventional signs,"
abstract gesture was still the emblem of the real.[4] He accepted
the concept of "artifice" in mime, which links him to the less
psychologically oriented stages of Paris Modern.

Although Marceau is not chronologically closest to Decroux,
he is ideologically and technically nearest to Decroux's early
work through the 1940s. Whereas Decroux went on to develop

new techniques and styles, Marceau has spent his career refining the illusionary form, and is responsible for its successful implementation in performance. He can be credited, along with Barrault, for having moved modern mime from the realm of theory to the theatrical forum. Although Marceau theorizes least, his approach to mime reflects the cerebral aesthetics of Paris Modern. Still operating are the principles of abstracting the essence of the real while maintaining reference points in the tangible world. Marceau abbreviates gesture to a greater degree that Decroux: His *raccourcis* are more refined. The structure of mime gesture for Marceau is fundamentally that of Decroux's early work. He has varied the content of mime by adding humor, sentiment, and caricature, as well as some imagistic numbers, that synthesize not only gesture, but time as well. Still, the sequential structure of reality remains unperverted. Gesture, for Marceau, is still denotative—meant to be interpreted literally, even if not performed literally. He, too, sustains the use of contrivance and artifice. Marceau relates to the early period of Paris Modern with its touchstones in reality.

In terms of Paris Modern, Barrault is the most significant of all the figures studied, as he represents a synthesis of all the major forces present in the aesthetics of the time. First, he is a theorizer and philosopher, reflecting the intellectual orientation of "the Paris style." Second, he accepts the fundamentals of the Decroux code and, with it, a particular orientation toward the abstract. What he does not accept is Decroux's isolation of mime from all other forms of expression; he sees mime only as one tool of the theater. He permits the word that expresses essential emotions. Barrault abstracts language and sounds as Decroux abstracted gesture. Interestingly, Barrault chose Faulkner's *As I Lay Dying* for his first mise en scène; of all American writers, it is Faulkner who is nearest to the Joycean style of Paris Modern.

Barrault is interested in man's animal drives, as well as his anima. In fact, the fundamental divergence between Decroux and Barrault is the influence of modern psychological theories on Barrault's aesthetics. This force leads him to delineate a gesture language other than Decroux's "objective" rendering of the illusion of reality. He labels this "subjective mime," for it is the external expression of the psyche and its primal needs. Barrault's mime-theater depicts the world of dreams and hal-

lucinations, the power of the subconscious and emotions, linking Barrault to expressionism, surrealism, and psychological
realism.

This psychological orientation of Barrault enables him to
perform successfully in film, which is a representational
medium. When Marceau performs on film, the magic of the
cinematic form overshadows the power of his illusions. The
only character Marceau can play is Marceau, the mime, hence
his lack of cinematic success. Contrast this to Barrault's performance in *Les Enfants du Paradis,* where he first creates the
character of the mime-actor Deburau, and then plays this psychologically developed character performing mime. He works
toward the development of subjective mimic gesture. Barrault's
addition of the "subjective" level of movement, moves modern
mime from the early to the middle period of Paris Modern.

Lecoq links up with Paris Modern at the point where Barrault
leaves off. Coming later in time, he rejects the Decroux code as
the definitive form and sees it only as a once necessary, but now
outdated phenomenon. He seeks instead the free and direct
expression of primal sensory states, thereby repudiating the
artifice of Decroux.

Lecoq believes that mime can attain total abstraction, that is,
seek no equivalency to tangible reality, portraying instead the
phantom forms of the subconscious. This nonrepresentational
gesture corresponds to the late stages of Paris Modern.

This mime can be combined with any form of theatrical expression provided that the actor maintains the sensory and
emotional immediacy of movement. Lecoq, like Barrault, believes that words and sounds when combined with mime must
express only essential needs.

Lecoq's mime is based on the liberation of the instincts. Para-
doxically enough, Lecoq, so devoted to freedom of expression,
has the most consistent, logical and comprehensive body of
theory of all the mimes studied. The aesthetic theorizing of
"the Paris style" holds its grip on even the last of these mimes.

Each of the four mimes relates to Paris Modern in an individual way, but each is definitely representative of some manifestation of this cultural phenomenon. It is clear that the entity
"modern French mime" exists as the corporeal expression of
contemporary aesthetics. It is not the mere prolongation of an
established tradition but a totally new form.

It is now fifty years since Decroux first set out to establish modern mime as a viable new art form. He clearly succeeded in reviving an art that appeared doomed to extinction. Today, in his eighties, he still teaches and gives private demonstrations of his virtuoso exercises. His son, Maximilien, continues the teaching of his father's theories, an occurrence strangely reminiscent of the troupes of ancient mimes, who passed the secrets of the art from father to son. Although the Decroux pedagogy has helped to mold hundreds of mimes, only Marceau and Barrault have captured the public's fancy. The hoards of Decroux disciples remain substantially unrecognized.

Marceau, now past his thirty-fifth year of virtuoso performances, continues to be the mime of greatest popular appeal. He has reached a vaster audience than any other mime in the history of the art. Years of activity remain before him. Although in recent years Marceau has devoted more time to his school in Paris, his protégés have not advanced the art beyond his own accomplishments. It is painful but realistic to say that the development of the illusionary mime grammar as an autonomous form probably reached its ultimate realization under Marceau and now appears at an impasse. The dead end predicted by Barrault years ago has come to pass.

Barrault still continues to insert mime effects into his theatrical performances. Despite the physical bias of his directing and acting styles, Barrault has advanced modern mime only in terms of its possible applications, but in recent years has done little to expand upon his early technical innovations. Barrault is unique among the four mimes, as he is the only one to claim no disciples, only a mass of admirers. He clearly has been less interested in the proselytization of the new mime than in the total development of his own unique talents. His work is marked by a constant exploration of forms and an unceasing attempt to expand his personal expressive abilities. Barrault's style renders him inimitable.

It is to Jacques Lecoq that one must turn for a projection of the new mime into new forms. Much of what is new in modern mime appears to be the work of Lecoq's protégés. This should not be viewed as the projection of a single line of force. The Lecoq training develops the mime in many diverse ways, and his disciples have chosen varying paths. His school continues to thrive as an international center for mime research, whereas the schools of Decroux and Marceau teach a preconceived technique. Although a few students of Decroux and Marceau apply the techniques with originality, most appear imprisoned by the rigidity of the imposed aesthetics. For this reason, Lecoq's mime remains the most open-ended of those studied.

It is interesting to note that although Decroux and Lecoq appear to have opposing theories, some of the second-generation mimes of each school seem to be moving in similar directions. It is no longer unusual to find a Decroux-trained mime exploring the Commedia dell'Arte. As modern French mime becomes an established art form, as performers become aware of differing approaches to the genre, mime artists will feel secure enough to synthesize techniques and concepts from various schools. Perhaps through this integration of styles, modern mime will find its new direction and surmount the impasse envisioned by Barrault.

As a consequence of the efforts of these four men, the art of mime has been spared. Decroux's campaign to prove to the twentieth century that this art could thrive again has culminated in a worldwide awakening of interest in the genre. To date, modern mime is still fundamentally linked to the names of these four pioneers of the art. It is to be hoped that more performers will achieve recognition in the future, so that modern mime can escape the rule of the past, under which the form perished with the great artist of each era.

Mime, throughout the centuries, has been clearly isolated from the so-called serious theater of each era. The concept of "total theater" as advanced by Copeau, Artaud, Barrault, Lecoq, and others, has developed an awareness of corporal expression as a viable theatrical tool. Mime no longer exists on the periphery of theater: the two forms are so often integrated that it has become increasingly difficult to distinguish between them. Many of the avant-garde theater groups of the 1960s and 1970s used mimetic techniques within their work: Joseph Chaikin's Open Theatre, André Gregory's Manhattan Project, Jerzy Grotowski's Polish Laboratory Theatre, Peter Brooks' Centre International de créations théâtrales; and more recently such shows as *The Regard of Flight with Bill Irwin* (American Place Theater, 1982), are among different manifestations of mime in theater. Today, the importance of mime technique is not in doubt, and it has become a fundamental component of actor training. The strictly autonomous mime of Decroux is a vestige of an early stage in the development of modern mime, when it needed to be isolated to be recognized as an art.

Contemporary mime has not totally repudiated its origins in Paris Modern. It continues a self-conscious view of itself as an art form. A growing number of publications on the subject appear every year. *Mime Journal,* begun in 1974, publishes articles on current and past mime aesthetics. In the same year the late Claude Kipnis, a mime of the Marceau school, wrote *The Mime Book,* a manual of stages of an action, a series of *attitudes* arranged as the individual frames of a motion picture; the reader, in flipping the pages, can see a sequence from Marceau's technique.[5] Illusions of walking in place, lifting, pulling, and pushing are explicated in so detailed a manner as to enable anyone who follows the simple directions to achieve the desired effect. One can only imagine Decroux's reaction to seeing his views popularized in such a manner. Nevertheless, the Kipnis book of mime recipes remains a logical final phase to Decroux's original work. Part of the code is now totally fixed, and while it provides a transmissible technique, it impedes creative and original expansion of thought.

The renewed interest in mime has caused the proliferation of mime schools and classes that teach various aspects of the mime tradition. This is clearly a twentieth-century phenomenon. The school for mimes of the past was family guidance and stage experience. Now mimes recognize an objective aesthetic standard; modern mime continues the self-awareness engendered by "the Paris style."

The development of modern mime begun fifty years ago has blossomed into a worldwide renaissance of an art once near extinction. Propelled by the desire to surpass denotative gesture, Etienne Decroux, Jean-Louis Barrault, Marcel Marceau, and Jacques Lecoq have strived to put mime in line with other twentieth-century art forms; in so doing, they have created a new mime genre. Born in silence, modern mime seeks its place in a world of words.

NOTES

Chapter 1. Introduction

1. *The Compact Edition of the Oxford English Dictionary* (New York: Oxford University Press, 1973), s.v. "mime":

mime sb. . . . 1. A performer in the dramatic pieces described in sense 4. . . .
2. A mimic, jester, buffoon; a pantomimist. . . .
3. An imitator. . . .
4. A kind of simple farce drama among the Greeks and Romans, characterized by mimicry and the ludicrous representation of familiar types of character; a dialogue written for recital in a performance of this kind. Also occasionally applied to similar performances in modern times. . . .
5. An imitation.
6. Mime-man, a mimic, mime v. . . . 1. To act or play a part with mimic gesture and action usually without words. . . .
2. To imitate, mimic. . . .

2. Aristotle, *The Poetics,* trans. G. M. A. Grube (New York: Bobbs Merrill, 1958), p. 11.

3. Allardyce Nicoll, *Masks, Mimes and Miracles* (New York: Cooper Square Publishers, 1963), p. 38.

4. Ibid., p. 45.

5. Ibid., p. 81.

6. Plato, *Collected Dialogues,* ed. Edith Hamilton and Huntington Cairns (New York, Billingen Foundation, 1961), p. 1256.

7. Jean Dorcy, *J'aime la mime* (Lausanne: Editions de noel, 1962), p. 45.

8. For a more detailed description of this process see Roger Garaudy, *Danser sa vie* (Paris: Seuil, 1973), pp. 17–19.

9. Marcel Mauss, *Manuel d'ethnographie* (Paris: Petite Bibliothèque Payot, 1967), p. 111.

10. Jacques Lecoq, "Le role de l'improvisation dans l'enseignement de l'art dramatique," transcript of lecture demonstration at the Institut International du Théâtre, Bucarest, 1964, p. 136.

11. For further discussion of the anthropology of gesture see Alison Jolly, *The evolution of Primate Behavior* (New York: MacMillan, 1972); Marcel Mauss, *Manuel d'ethnographie;* and Marcel Jousse, *L'Anthropologie du geste* (Paris: Resma, 1960).

12. Richard Southern speculates on the evolution from ritual and communication to theatre art in *The Seven Ages of the Theatre* (New York: Hill & Wang, 1963), pp. 21–34.

13. Dorcy, *J'aime la mime*, p. 45.

14. Gaston Charles Vuillier, cited in *Meyerhold on Theatre*, trans. and ed. Edward Braun (New York: Hill & Wang, 1969), p. 124.

15. Constant Mic, *La Commedia dell'Arte* (Paris: La Pléiade, 1927), p. 120.

16. Ibid., p. 117.

17. Pierre Louis Duchartre, *The Italian Comedy* (New York: Dover Publications, 1966), p. 25.

18. Ibid., p. 243.

19. Giacomo Oreglia, *The Commedia dell'Arte* (New York: Hill & Wang, 1968), p. 114.

20. For a complete history of the Commedia dell'Arte in France see Gustav Attinger, *L'esprit de la Commedia dell'Arte dans le théâtre français* (Paris: Librarie theatrale, 1950); and Duchartre, *The Italian Comedy*.

21. See David Mayer, *Harlequin in his Element* (Cambridge: Harvard University Press, 1969) for documentation of these scenarios.

22. Multiple plots were long part of English written drama. It is possible that this tradition was merely carried over into the pantomime style.

23. For complete biographic data see Richard Findlater, *Grimaldi: King of Clowns* (London: MacGibbon and Kee; 1955).

24. Findlater makes the distinction between "Clown" and "clown" in *Grimaldi King of Clowns*, p. 12.

25. Tristan Rémy, *Jean-Gaspard Deburau* (Paris: L'Arche Editeur, 1954) documents these petitions.

26. For complete biographic data see Rémy, *Deburau*, and Jules Janin, *Deburau* (Paris: Librarie des Bibliophiles, 1881).

27. The evolution of Pierrot is documented by Maurice Sand, Kay Dick, Paul Hugonet, and Pierre Louis Duchartre.

28. Kay Dick, *Pierrot* (London: Hutchinson, 1960), p. 30.

29. Théophile Gautier, cited in Tristan Rémy, *Jean-Gaspard Deburau* (Paris: L'Arche Editeur, 1954), pp. 167–68.

30. Dick, *Pierrot*, p. 170.

31. Rémy, *Jean-Gaspard Duburau*, p. 212.

32. George Sand, cited in Maurice Sand, *Masques et Buffons* (Paris: Michel Lévy Frères, 1960), p. 295.

33. Rémy, *Jean-Gaspard Deburau*, p. 196.

34. Victor Leathers, *British Entertainers in France*, (Toronto: University of Toronto Press, 1959), pp. 128–29.

35. Sand, *Masques of Buffons*, p. 295.

36. Ibid., p. 295.

37. Louis Péricaud, *Le Théâtre des funambules* (Paris: Léon Sapin Librarie, 1897), p. 292.

38. Rémy, *Jean-Gaspard Deburau*, pp. 176–77.

39. Paul Hugounet, *Mimes and Pierrots* (Paris: Librarie Fischbacher, 1889), p. 120.

40. Charles Dullin, *Souvenirs et notes de travail d'un Acteur* (Paris: Odette Lieutier, 1946), p. 127.

41. Ibid., p. 128.

42. The monolithic face of actors like Buster Keaton can create the impression of a mask.

Chapter 2. Jacques Copeau

1. Jacques Copeau, "An Essay of Dramatic Renovation," trans. Richard Hiatt, *Educational Theatre Journal*, no. 19, (December 1967).
2. For Copeau's notes on his visit with Craig, see Copeau, "Visites a Gordon Craig, Jaques-Dalcroze et Adolphe Appia," *Revue d'histoire du Théâtre*, 15e année, (December 1963), pp. 357–67.
3. Copeau, cited in Marcel Doisy, *Jacques Copeau*, (Paris: Le cercle du Livre, 1954), p. 107.
4. For further information on Craig's ideas, see: *The Mask* (Florence, Italy) I, no. 1 (April 1908).
5. For Copeau's notes on his visit with Dalcroze, see "Visites," pp. 367–70.
6. Copeau, "Visites," p. 373.
7. For Copeau's notes on his visit with Appia, see "Visites," pp. 371–74.
8. Clement Borgal, *Jacques Copeau*, (Paris: L'Arche Editeur, 1960), p. 123.
9. Ibid., pp. 123–24.
10. Copeau, "Visites," p. 374.
11. Jacques Copeau, *Souvenirs du Vieux Colombier*, (Paris: Nouvelles Editions Latines, 1931), p. 51.
12. Ibid., p. 52.
13. The Montessori nursery was run by the wife of critic-writer Waldo David Frank.
14. Maurice Kurtz, *Jacques Copeau: Biographie d'un Théâtre*, (Paris: Les Editions Nagel, 1950), pp. 66–67.
15. Copeau, *Souvenirs*, pp. 92–93.
16. George Hebert, *L'Education physique ou l'entrainement complet par la méthode naturelle*, 5 vols. (Paris: Librarie Vuibert, 1912).
17. Jean Dorcy, Private interview, Paris, February 1972.
18. Suzanne Bing, cited in Barbara Leigh Kusler "Jacques Copeau's School for Actors," *Mime Journal*, nos. 9 and 10 (1979).
19. Ibid., p. 21.
20. Kurtz, *Jacques Copeau*, p. 63.
21. Kusler, "Jacques Copeau's School," p. 13.
22. Kusler, "Jacques Copeau's School," p. 13, and Kurtz, *Jacques Copeau*, p. 63.
23. Kusler, "Jacques Copeau's School," p. 32.
24. Ibid., p. 32.
25. Ibid., p. 18.
26. Ibid., p. 44.
27. For further information, see Sears Eldredge, "Jacques Copeau and the Mask in Actor Training," *Mime, Mask, and Marionette*, 2, nos. 3–4 (1979–1980).
28. Copeau, *Souvenirs*, p. 92.
29. Copeau, "Réflexions d'un comédien sur le 'Paradoxe de Diderot,'" *Ecrits sur le théâtre*, (Paris: Michel Brient Editeur, 1955), pp. 25–26.
30. Jean Dorcy, *J'aime la mime*, (Lausanne: Editions de noël, 1962), p. 51.

31. Waldo Frank, "Copeau Begins Again," *Theatre Arts Monthly*, no. 9 (September 1925), p. 588.

32. Copeau, "Notes sur l'éducation de l'acteur," *Ecrits*, pp. 47–53.

33. Jean Dorcy, *The Mime*, trans. Robert Speller, Jr. and Pierre de Fontnouvelle (New York: Robert Speller, 1961), pp. 108–9.

34. Interview with Jean Dorcy, Paris, 1972.

35. Kusler, "Jacques Copeau's School," p. 31.

36. Dorcy, Interview.

37. Frank, "Copeau Begins Again," pp. 588–89.

38. Copeau, *Souvenirs*, p. 76.

39. Letter from Copeau to Louis Jouvet, cited in Kurtz, *Jacque Copeau*, p. 68.

40. Kusler, "Jacques Copeau's School," p. 31.

41. Several of Copeau's plays using choral movement and Commedia style were revised by Jean Dasté. Among them—*L'Illusion*, 1950, and *Arlequin Magicien*, 1941.

42. Copeau, *Souvenirs*, p. 99.

43. André Gide, cited in Eric Bentley, *In Search of Theatre*, (New York: Alfred A. Knopf, 1953), p. 259.

44. Louis Jouvet and Charles Dullin who began their acting careers at the Vieux-Colombier and acknowledged their debt to Copeau for imparting an understanding of pantomime and improvisation as the key to their craft; Michel Saint-Denis, Copeau's nephew, who inherited the leadership of Copeau's students upon his uncle's retirement and continued the traditions of his mentor as head of the Companie des Quinze (a group of fifteen of Copeau's students and faculty), and later became head of the Old Vic Theatre School where he established a curriculum based on that of the Vieux-Colombier; and Jean Dasté, Copeau's son-in-law, headed several theater companies that performed a repertory comprised of Molière, and other Commedia-based classics, masked *mimodrames*, and adaptations of Noh plays.

45. Jean-Louis Barrault, *Souvenirs pour demain* (Paris: Edition du Seuil, 1972), p. 64.

46. Antonin Artaud, *The Theatre and its Double*, trans. Mary Caroline Richards (New York: Grove Press, 1958), pp. 37–40.

Chapter 3. Etienne Decroux

1. Thomas Leabhart, "An Interview with Etienne Decroux," *Mime Journal* 1 (1974): 29.

2. Etienne Decroux, *Paroles sur le mime* (Paris: Gallimard, 1963), p. 13.

3. Vernice Klier, "Etienne Decroux 80th Birthday Interview," *Mime Journal* 7 and 8 (1978): 62.

4. Leabhart, "An Interview with Etienne Decroux," 28.

5. Alvin Epstein, "The Mime Theatre of Etienne Decroux," *Chrysalis* 11, no. 1–2 (1958): 6.

6. Ibid., p. 6.

7. Annette Lust, "Etienne Decroux, Father of Modern Mime," *Mime Journal* 1 (1974): 16.

8. Interestingly enough, the activities portrayed in *La Vie Primitive* and *La*

Vie Médiévale correspond directly to the volume titles in Hébert's series of books on physical education: *Grimper* (Climbing), *Lancer* (Throwing), *Défense* (Combat). In these books, Hébert gives diagrams of the natural method for performing these acts. There is a systematic depiction of each step necessary to complete an action (a presentation similar to the images in individual frames of a motion picture). Following the Hébert directions would have enabled a mime to perform these acts in perfect economy. Since Copeau gave courses in Hébertisme, this appears to be one more case of Decroux's "adding" to the exercises used at the Vieux Colombier, actually building a performance out of the embryonic forms presented there.

9. Eric Bentley, *In Search of Theatre* (New York: Alfred A. Knopf, 1953), p. 187.

10. Jean-Louis Barrault, *Réflexions sur le théâtre* (Paris: J. Vautrain, 1949), p. 34.

11. Decroux, quoted in Thomas Leabhart, "Etienne Decroux on Masks," *Mime Journal* 2 (1975): 56.

12. Barrault, *Réflexions sur le Théâtre*, p. 35.

13. Ibid.

14. Ibid., p. 36.

15. Ibid., pp. 37–39.

16. Ibid., p. 36.

17. Decroux, *Paroles sur le mime*, p. 147.

18. Barrault, *Réflexions sur le théâtre*, p. 39.

19. Jean Dorcy, *A la rencontre de mime et des mimes* (Neuilly sur Seine: Les Cahiers de Danse et de Culture, 1958), p. 71.

20. Ibid., p. 66.

21. Dorcy, "Jean-Louis Barrault et Etienne Decroux, créateurs du mime corporel," *Gavroche* (Nimes), 26 July 1945.

22. Jean-Louis Barrault, *Souvenirs pour demain* (Paris, Editions de Seuil, 1972), p. 72.

23. Decroux, *Paroles sur le mime*, p. 147.

24. Ibid., p. 144.

25. Ibid., p. 18.

26. Epstein, "The Mime Theatre of Etienne Decroux," p. 9.

27. Ibid., p. 8.

28. Decroux, *Paroles sur le mime*, p. 60.

29. Etienne Decroux quoted in Pierre Richy and J-C. de Mauraige, *Initiation au mime* (Paris: Editions Amicales, 1968), p. 24.

30. Leabhart, "Etienne Decroux on Masks," p. 58.

31. Decroux, *Paroles sur le mime*, p. 60.

32. Leabhart, "Etienne Decroux on Masks," p. 58.

33. Ibid., pp. 57–58.

34. Ibid., p. 56.

35. Ibid., p. 56.

36. Ibid., p. 59.

37. It should be noted that Picasso, Braque, Derain, DeChirico, Miro, and Ernst, among others were designing stage sets in Paris in the 1920s while Decroux was in the early stages of developing his mime theory.

38. Picasso's *Woman's Head*, ca. 1909, is almost identical to Decroux's description of the prismed mask, in which each facet casts a shadow, creating a

play of light and movement.

39. Leabhart, "Etienne Decroux on Masks," p. 60.

40. Ibid.

41. There is a traditional fool's mask that can be traced from ancient Greece through Rome to the Commedia, that represents particular human foibles. Similar traditional masks exist for other characters.

42. Decroux, *Paroles sur le mime,* pp. 19–28.

43. Edward Gordon Craig, "To Madame Eleonora Duse," *The Mask* 1 (March 1908): 8–9.

44. Craig, "The Actor and the Uber-marionette," *The Mask* 1 (April 1908): 7.

45. Craig visited the Vieux Colombier when Decroux was a student there, and more than twenty years later visited the Ecole Decroux, where he lauded the accomplishments of Decroux's mime theories in practice. These two men mutually appreciated each other's work.

46. Decroux, *Paroles sur le mime,* p. 21.

47. Decroux quoted in Thomas Leabhart, "The Origin of Corporeal Mime," *Mime Journal* 7 and 8 (1975): 15.

48. Bentley, *In Search of Theatre,* p. 187.

49. Decroux, *Paroles, sur le mime* p. 180.

50. Etienne Decroux, Zélateur du mime," *Spectateur,* 12 November 1946.

51. Decroux, quoted in Georges Ravon, *Figaro Littéraire,* 27 March 1954.

52. William Fleming, *Arts and Ideas* (New York: Holt Rinehart & Winston, 1963), p. 381.

53. Lust, "Etienne Decroux, Father of Modern Mime," p. 20.

54. Jean Dorcy, "Jean-Louis Barrault et Etienne Decroux," *Gavroche* (Nimes), 26 July 1945.

55. Ibid.

56. Yves Lebreton, "Entretien: Yves Lebreton," *Empreintes* 4 (1980): 64.

57. Ibid., p. 65.

58. Kari Margolis and Tony Brown, Private interview, New York, October 1982.

59. Ibid.

60. Decroux, *Paroles sur le mime,* p. 76.

61. Lily and Baird Hastings, "The New Mime of Etienne Decroux," *Dance,* September 1951, p. 14.

62. Leabhart, "An Interview with Etienne Decroux," p. 28.

63. Bentley, *In Search of Theatre,* pp. 190–91.

64. Roger Garaudy, *Danser sa vie* (Paris: Editions du Seuil, 1973), p. 23.

65. Ibid., pp. 23–24.

66. Lust, "Etienne Decroux, Father of Modern Mime," p. 19.

67. Dorcy, *J'aime la mime,* p. 62.

68. Decroux, *Paroles sur le mime,* pp. 49–50.

69. Bentley, *In Search of Theatre,* p. 189.

70. Ibid., p. 194.

71. Gaston Baty, quoted in Helène Garcin, "Etienne Decroux," *Aujourd'hui* (Paris), 25 May 1942.

72. Hubert Engelhard, "Le mime Etienne Decroux," *Réforme,* 31 May 1947.

73. Claude Outie, "Decroux, Comédien sans visage," *Combat,* 19 June 1946.

74. Engelhard, "Le mime Etienne Decroux."

75. Walter Kerr, "Etienne Decroux Stages 'Mime Theatre' Program," *New York Herald Tribune*, 24 December 1959.

76. Frances Herridge, "Decroux Mime Theatre at Cricket," *New York Post*, 24 December 1959.

77. Dorcy, *A la rencontre de mime et des mimes*, p. 73.

78. Jean-Louis Barrault, Interview by William Weiss and Daniele Marty, Paris, January 1972.

79. Engelhard, "Le mime Etienne Decroux."

80. Arthur Gelb, "Theatre: Pantomime Art," *New York Times*, 12 December 1959.

81. Norman Nadel, "Mime Theatre of Decroux in Carnegie Recital Hall," *New York World Telegram and Sun*, 8 November 1961.

82. Robert J. Landry, "Paris Dean of Mime at Actors' Studio," *Variety*, 23 October 1957.

83. Herridge, "Decroux Mime Theatre at Cricket," *New York Post*, 24 December 1959.

84. Kerr, "Etienne Decroux Stages Mime Theatre Program," *New York Herald Tribune*, 24 December 1959.

85. Leabhart, "An Interview with Etienne Decroux," p. 33.

86. Interview with Kari Margolis and Tony Brown, 1982.

87. Lebreton, "Entretien: Yves Lebreton," pp. 62–63.

88. Daniel Dobbels, "Entretien: Yves Marc, Claire Heggen," *Empreintes* 4 (1980): 69.

89. Thomas Leabhart, Private interview, New York, August 1982.

90. Lebreton, "Entretien: Yves Lebreton," p. 63.

91. Jean Dorcy, Private interview, Paris, February 1972.

92. Daniel Dobbels, "Entretien: Jean-Louis Barrault," *Empreintes* 4 (1980): 51.

93. Bentley, *In Search of Theatre*, p. 195.

94. *Ibid.*, p. 193.

Chapter 4. Jean-Louis Barrault

1. Company founded by Barrault following his apprenticeship at the Atelier.

2. Jean-Louis Barrault, *Souvenirs pour demain* (Paris: Editions du Seuil, 1972), p. 105.

3. *Ibid.*, p. 70.

4. Jean-Louis Barrault, Interview by William Weiss and Daniele Marty, Paris, January 1972.

5. Paolo Emilio Poesio, "Jean-Louis Barrault," *Documenti di teatro*, no. 17, p. 22.

6. Barrault, Interview, January 1972.

7. Jean Dorcy, "Jean-Louis Barrault et Etienne Decroux," *Gavroche* (Nimes), 26 July 1945.

8. Barrault, quoted in Jean Dorcy, *A la rencontre de mime et des mimes* (Neuilly sur Seine: Les Cahiers de danse et de culture, 1958), p. 80.

9. Daniel Dobbels, "Entretien de Jean-Louis Barrault," *Empreintes*, no. 4 (January 1980), p. 50.

10. Barrault, *Souvenirs pour demain,* pp. 102–114.

11. Antonin Artaud, *The Theatre and its Double,* trans. Mary Caroline Richards (New York: Grove Press, 1958), p. 12.

12. Ibid., p. 54.

13. Ibid., p. 123.

14. Ibid., p. 46.

15. Ibid., p. 38.

16. Barrault, Interview, January 1972.

17. Jean-Louis Barrault, *The Theatre of Jean-Louis Barrault* (London: Barrie and Rockliff, 1961), pp. 29–30.

18. Artaud, *The Theatre and its Double,* p. 44.

19. Annette Lust, "Etienne Decroux, Father of Modern Mime," *Mime Journal* 1 (1974): 19–20.

20. Barrault, *Reflections on the Theatre* (London: Rockliff Publishing, 1951), p. 157.

21. Barrault, *Réflexions sur le théâtre* (Paris: J. Vautrain, 1949), p. 39.

22. Poesio, "Jean-Louis Barrault," p. 7.

23. Barrault, *Nouvelles réflexions sur le théâtre* (Paris: Flammarion, 1959), p. 76.

24. Ibid., p. 82.

25. Ibid., p. 45.

26. Dorcy, *A la recontre de mime et des mimes* (Neuilly sur Seine: Les cahiers de danse et de culture, 1958), p. 129.

27. Barrault, *Réflexions sur le théâtre,* p. 39.

28. Barrault, *Nouvelles réflexions sur le théâtre,* p. 75.

29. Ibid., p. 82.

30. Barrault, Interview, January 1972.

31. Barrault, *Nouvelles réflexions sur le théâtre,* pp. 78–79.

32. Ibid., p. 79.

33. Ibid., pp. 80–81.

34. Ibid., p. 81.

35. Ibid., p. 81.

36. Ibid., p. 82.

37. Barrault, *Réflexions sur le théâtre,* p. 36.

38. Barrault, *Souvenirs pour demain,* p. 107. A similar description of the *Kabbale* can be found in Artaud, *The Theatre and its Double,* pp. 136–38.

39. Ibid., p. 107.

40. Ibid., pp. 108–9.

41. Ibid., p. 107.

42. Ibid., p. 110.

43. Dobbels, "Entretien de Barrault," p. 52.

44. Barrault, *Souvenirs pour demain,* p. 110.

45. Ibid., p. 106.

46. Ibid., p. 86.

47. Ibid., p. 84.

48. Dobbels, "Entretien de Barrault," p. 51.

49. Barrault, *Souvenirs pour demain,* p. 89.

50. Antonin Artaud, "Autour d'une mère," *La Nouvelle Revue Française,* July 1935, p. 136.

51. Barrault, *The Theatre of Jean-Louis Barrault,* p. 36.

52. Barrault, *Reflections on the Theatre*, p. 35.
53. Ibid., p. 39.
54. Artaud, *The Theatre and its Double*, p. 46.
55. Barrault, *Souvenirs pour demain*, p. 85.
56. Stern, "Autour d'une mère," *Variety*, 19 June 1935.
57. Ibid.
58. Artaud, *"Autour d'une mère,"* p. 136.
59. Artaud, *The Theatre and its Double*, p. 33.
60. Barrault, *Souvenirs pour demain*, p. 105.
61. Artaud, *"Autour d'une mère,"* p. 136.
62. Poesio, "Jean-Louis Barrault," p. 33.
63. Louis Jouvet, quoted in Barrault, *Souvenirs pour demain*, p. 90.
64. Barrault, *Souvenirs pour demain*, p. 91.
65. Barrault, Interview, January 1972.
66. "Jean-Louis Barrault et Madeleine Renaud reçoivent," ORTF, radio, May 1974.
67. Poesio, "Jean-Louis Barrault," p. 159.
68. Philip Carr, "Paris Looks at Spain," *New York Times*, 13 June 1937.
69. Eric Bentley, ed. *The Classic Theatre*, (Garden City, N. Y.: Doubleday, Anchor Books, 1959), p. 482.
70. Pierre Brisson, *"Numance,"* *Le Figaro*, 25 April 1937.
71. George Altman, "Drame d'un peuple, *Numance,*" *Le Peuple*, 4 May 1937.
72. Stefan Priacol, "Après 350 ans-*Numance,*" *Humanité*, 4 May 1937.
73. Altman, "Drame d'un peuple, *Numance,*" *Le Peuple*, 4 May 1937.
74. Barrault, *Souvenirs pour demain*, p. 113.
75. Altman, "Drame d'un peuple, *Numance,*" *Le Peuple*, 4 May 1937.
76. Barrault, *Souvenirs pour demain*, p. 122.
77. *Ibid*, p. 70.
78. Jean-Louis Barrault, quoted in Brisson, *"Numance,"* *Le Figaro*, 25 April 1937.
79. Brisson, "Numance."
80. Barrault, *Souvenirs pour demain*, p. 89.
81. Jean-Louis Barrault, "La Faim," *Le Jour*, 9 April 1939.
82. Jean-Louis Barrault, "Entretiens sur le Théâtre," *La Revue Théâtrale*, 7ᵉ année, no. 19 (1952).
83. Antoine, *"Hamlet* et *la Faim," Journal*, 20 April 1939.
84. Pierre Brisson, *"La Faim,"* *Le Figaro*, 23 April 1939.
85. "Spectacle J-L. Barrault à l'Atelier," *L'Oeuvre*, 28 April 1939.
86. Benjamin Cremieux, "Hamlet et Le Faim, au Théâtre de l'Atelier," *La Lumière*, 5 May 1939.
87. Artaud, *The Theatre and its Double*, p. 89.
88. Barrault, *Souvenirs pour demain*, p. 84.
89. Cremieux, *"Hamlet* et *La Faim* au Théâtre de l'Atelier," 5 May 1939.
90. *"Hamlet* et *La Faim," L'Oeuvre*, 28 April 1939.
91. Barrault, *Souvenirs pour demain*, p. 125.
92. Artaud, *The Theatre and its Double*, p. 92.
93. Barrault, *Souvenirs pour demain*, p. 70.
94. Antoine, *"Hamlet* et *La Faim," Journal*, 20 April 1939.
95. Brisson, La Faim," *Le Figaro*, 23 April 1939.
96. *"Hamlet* et *La Faim"* *Lumière*, 5 May 1939.
97. Lucien Descaves, *"La Faim,"* *Intran*, 20 April 1939.

98. "*Hamlet* et *La Faim*," *Gringoire*, 11 May 1939.

99. Barrault, "Entretiens sur le théâtre," *La Revue Théâtrale*, no. 19 (1952), p. 13.

100. Ibid.

101. Barrault, *The Theatre of Jean-Louis Barrault*, p. 29.

102. Barrault, "Entretiens sur le théâtre," p. 13.

103. Barrault, *Réflexions sur le théâtre*, p. 175.

104. Armand Salacrou, Preface to Barrault's *Nouvelles réflexions sur le théâtre*, p. 8.

105. Barrault, *Souvenirs pour demain*, p. 145.

106. Barrault, *The Theatre of Jean-Louis Barrault*, p. 30.

107. Barrault, *Réflexions sur le théâtre*, p. 176.

108. Holhannes I. Pilikan, "Dialogue with Barrault," *Drama* 89 (Summer 1968).

109. Dobbels, "Entretien de Barrault," p. 53.

110. Barrault, *Nouvelles réflexions sur le théâtre*, p. 73.

111. Barrault, Interview, January 1972.

112. Barrault, *The Theatre of Jean-Louis Barrault*, p. 30.

113. Barrault, *Nouvelles réflexions sur le théâtre*, p. 72.

114. Barrault, *Réflexions sur le théâtre*, p. 175.

115. Barrault, cited in Eric Bentley, *In Search of Theatre* (New York: Alfred A. Knopf, 1953), p. 262.

116. Jacques Copeau, *Appels* (Paris: Gallimard, 1974), p. 115.

117. Jon Carlson, "Reducible to a Single Presence," *Village Voice*, 28 May 1970.

Chapter 5. Marcel Marceau

1. Marc Beigbeder, "Bip repetita placent," *Lettres Françaises*, 10 June 1954.

2. Program, Edenburgh International Festival, 1967.

3. Beigbeder, "Bip repetita placent."

4. Barrault has an interesting anecdote to recount. "I held auditions for the role of Harlequin, after which I retained two young men: Maurice Béjart and Marcel Marceau. I chose Marceau who was thinner and more flexible. . . . Later Béjart confided in me that this choice decided his career. What luck for him and for us." Jean-Louis Barrault, *Souvenirs pour demain*, p. 195.

5. Guy Dornand, "Marcel Marceau et ses pantomimes," *Libération*, 1 June 1953.

6. Marcel Marceau, quoted in Pierre Richy, *Jeu Silencieux* (Editions Amicales: Paris, 1969), p. 4.

7. Ibid. For further discussion of the intransmissible nature of mime, see chapter I.

8. Marcel Marceau, "L'art de la mime," *Théâtre de L'Ambigu, rélations avec la presse*, 1956.

9. Ibid.

10. *The Mime of Marcel Marceau*, Learning Corporation of America, 1972.

11. Robert Kemp, "Marcel Marceau à L'Ambigu," *Le Monde*, 11 May 1956.

12. François Paglio, *Temps Chrétien*, 8 June 1956.

13. Presumably Marceau is referring to Webster's dictionary.

14. Marcel Marceau, "The Art of Mime," Publicity Release by Ronald Wilford Associates, U.S.A., 1955.

15. Christian Megret, "Etonnant Marceau," *Carrefour*, 9 October 1958.

16. Stephane Vallaire, "Marcel Marceau, Maissoneur de l'espace," *Lettres Françaises*, 9 October 1958.

17. Clive Barnes, "Marceau's Lyric Poems of Movement," *New York Times*, 6 April 1975.

18. Jacques Marchand, *Le Figaro*, 5 July 1952.

19. Marcel Marceau, Lecture-Demonstration, Brooklyn College, May 1973.

20. Ibid.

21. Ibid.

22. Marceau, Lecture-Demonstration, Théâtre des Nations Festival, Paris, April 1972.

23. Marceau, quoted in Rebecca Cox, "Marcel Marceau Speaks," *Prompt*, no. 11 (1968), p. 10.

24. Constantin Stanislavski, *An Actor Prepares* (Harmondsworth, Middlesex: Penguin Books, 1967), pp. 25–26.

25. Cox, "Marcel Marceau Speaks," p. 10.

26. R. G. Davis, "Method in Mime," *Tulane Drama Review* 6, no. 4 (Summer 1962): 61.

27. Marceau, quoted in Alan Bunce, "French Emissary of Mime," *The Christian Science Monitor*, 8 May 1970.

28. Marceau, cited in Bunce, "French Emissary of Mime."

29. Jean Dorcy, *A la rencontre de mime et des mimes* (Neuilly sur seine: Les cahiers de danse et de culture, 1958), p. 139.

30. Marcel Marceau, "Voici mes publics," *Arts*, 11 April 1956.

31. Jacques Marchand, *Le Figaro*, 5 July 1952.

32. "Le retour de Marcel Marceau," *Lettres Françaises*, 27 May 1954.

33. Jean-Louis Barrault, *The Theatre of Jean-Louis Barrault* (London: Rockliff Publishing, 1961), pp. 29–30.

34. Guy Dornand, "Marcel Marceau ou: le triomphe du Silence," *La Libération*, 14 May 1956.

35. Robert Kemp, "Marcel Marceau à l'Ambigu," *Le Monde*, 11 May 1956.

36. Roche, "Marcel Marceau," *Ce Soir,*. 12 August 1947.

37. Ibid.

38. R. G. Davis, "Method in Mime," *Tulane Drama Review* 6, no. 4 (Summer 1963), p. 63.

39. Ibid., p. 62.

40. Marceau, quoted in Cox, "Marcel Marceau Speaks," p. 10.

41. Charles Chaplin, *My Autobiography* (New York: Simon & Schuster, 1964), p. 95.

42. Marceau, "The Language of the Heart," American Publicity Release, Ronald Wilford Associates, New York, 1955.

43. Marceau quoted in Cox, "Marcel Marceau Speaks," p. 9.

44. Ibid., p. 10.

45. Marcel Marceau, "L'art du mime et de la pantomime," Program, Théâtre de la Comédie, Geneva, November 9 and 10, 1954.

46. Marceau, quoted in Jaqueline Cartier, "Marceau: Un art qui a les pieds sur le sol," 1958.

47. Marceau, quoted in Cox, "Marcel Marceau Speaks."

48. Dorcy, "A la rencontre de mime et des mimes," p. 96.

49. Marcel Marceau, "Pierrot de Montmartre," *Arts,* 19 June 1952.

50. Ibid.

51. Ibid.

52. Jean Dorcy offers a partial list of these pantomimes; see *A la rencontre de mime et des mimes,* pp. 96–97.

53. "Renouveau de la Pantomime", *La Croix,* 15 April 1950.

54. "La companie Marcel Marceau a installé Bip dans ses meubles," *Action,* 16 April 1950.

55. Marcel Marceau, "Pierrot de Montmartre," *Arts,* 19 June 1952.

56. André Ransan, "Studio des Champs Elysées, Spectacle de Pantomime," *Ce Matin le Pays,* 12 March 1951.

57. Marceau quoted in Cartier, "Marceau: Un art qui a les pieds sur le sol."

58. Jean-Jacques Gautier, "A L'Ambigu, le mime Marceau et sa companie," *Le Figaro,* 4 May 1956.

59. Clive Barnes, "Marceau's Lyric Poems of Movement," *New York Times,* 6 April 1975.

60. "Au Théâtre de la Renaissance, Marcel Marceau," *Le Figaro,* 5 June 1954.

61. B. de Garambé, "Le Mime Marcel Marceau enchaine la lune et la terre," *Le Théâtre,* 10 June 1954.

62. Pierre Marcam, "Marcel Marceau L'espirit avant le coeur," *Arts,* 8 October 1958.

63. Le Figaro Littéraire, 23 June 1956.

64. Ibid.

65. André Alter, "Marcel Marceau nous restitue l'art du mime dans toute sa plénitude," *L'Aube,* 19 April 1950.

66. Marceau quoted in Bunce, "French Emissary of Mime."

67. Ibid.

68. Ibid.

69. Paul Guth, *Le Figaro Littéraire,* 23 June 1956.

70. Marcel Marceau, *Program,* Saville Theatre, "The Origins of Bip," 2, no. 11 (1967).

71. Guth, *Le Figaro Littéraive.*

72. Marceau, quoted in Cox, "Marcel Marceau Speaks," p. 10.

73. Ibid., p. 10.

74. Pierre Louis Duchartre, *The Italian Comedy* (New York: Dover Publications, 1966), pp. 252–253; Allardyce Nicoll, *Masks, Mimes, and Miracles* (New York: Cooper Square Publishers, 1963), pp. 294–295.

75. Marceau himself has written *The Story of Bip* (New York: Harper & Row, 1976).

76. "Renouveau de la pantomime," *La Croix,* 15 April 1950.

77. Marceau, "Un qui se tait," *Arts,* 21 April 1950.

78. Brooks Atkinson "Theatre—Marcel Marceau," *New York Times,* 22 September 1955.

79. Ibid.

80. de Garambé, "Le Mime Marcel Marceau."

81. Martin Gottfried, "Marceau Quietly Returns" *New York Post,* 26 March 1975.

82. Walter Terry, "The Dance World, Marceau's Miming," February 1956.

83. "Renouveau de la pantomime," *La Croix*, 15 April 1950.

84. de Garambé, "Le Mime Marcel Marceau."

85. Marceau, quoted in Cox, "Marcel Marceau Speaks," p. 10.

86. Jean Pelleautier, "Un film sur l'art du silence," *Lettres Françaises*, 25 December 1954.

87. Pierre Marcabru, "Le Mime Marcel Marceau," *Arts*, 23–29 May 1956.

88. A. H. Weiler, "Marceau in Dual Roles in *Shanks*," *New York Times*, 10 October 1974.

89. Marceau quoted in Cox, "Marcel Marceau Speaks," p. 10.

90. Gottfried, "Marceau Quietly Returns."

91. Ibid.

92. Clive Barnes, "Marceau's Lyric Poems of Movement," *New York Times*, 6 April 1975.

93. Aljean Harnetz, "Marcel Marceau—Look Ma, He's Talking," *New York Times*, 25 November 1973.

Chapter 6. Jacques Lecoq

1. Jean Dorcy, *A la rencontre de mime et des mimes*, (Neuilly sur Seine: Les Cahiers de Dance et de Culture, 1958), p. 38.

2. Ibid., p. 38.

3. Ibid., p. 39.

4. "Voyage autour du Mime," Program Teatro Quirino, March 26, 1959.

5. Ibid.

6. Allardyce Nicoll, *Masks, Mimes and Miracles* (New York: Cooper Square Publishers, 1963), p. 81.

7. Aristotle, *On Poetry and Style*, trans. G. M. A. Grube (New York: Bobbs-Merrill, 1958), p. 7.

8. Jacques Lecoq, "L'école Jacques Lecoq," *Théâtre de la Ville*, no. 15 (January 1972), p. 41.

9. Ibid., p. 9.

10. Marcel Jousse, *L'anthropologie du geste* (Paris: Resma, 1960), p. 52.

11. Ibid., p. 54.

12. Alison Jolly, *The Evolution of Primate Behavior* (New York: Macmillan, 1972), p. 340.

13. Lecoq, "L'école Jacques Lecoq," p. 41.

14. Ibid., p. 41.

15. Etienne Decroux, *Paroles sur le mime* (Paris: Gallimard, 1963), p. 114.

16. Lecoq, "L'école Jacques Lecoq," p. 41.

17. Ralph L. Beals and Harry Hoijer, *An Introduction to Anthropology* (New York: MacMillan, 1964), p. 574.

18. Jacques Lecoq, "Le mouvement et le théâtre," *ATAC Info*, no. 13, (December 1967).

19. Jolly, *The Evolution of Primate Behavior*, pp. 142–145, p. 340.

20. Lecoq, "Le mouvement et le théâtre."

21. Jacques Lecoq, Personal notes, Stage d'été, 1971.

22. Lecoq, "L'ecole Jacques Lecoq," p. 42.

23. Jacques Lecoq, Private interview, Paris, May 1972.

24. Lecoq, Stage d'été, 1971, notes.

25. Beals and Hoijer, *An Introduction to Anthropology*, p. 573.

26. Alison Jolly, *The Evolution of Primate Behavior*, p. 145.

27. Georges Mounin, *Introduction à la sémiologie*, (Paris: les éditions de minuit, 1970), p. 175.

28. Carl C. Jung, "Approaching the Unconscious," *Man and his Symbols* (New York: Dell, 1968), p. 61.

29. Jacques Lecoq, quoted in Georges Mounin, *Introduction à la sémiologie* (Paris: les éditions de minuit, 1970), p. 175.

30. Mounin, *Introduction à la sémiologie*, pp. 179–180.

31. Decroux, *Paroles sur le mime*, p. 114.

32. Bari Rolfe, "Masks, Mimes and Mummenschanz," *Mime Journal*, no. 2. (1975), p. 25.

33. Aniela Jaffe, "Symbolism in the Visual Arts," in *Man and His Symbols*, ed. Carl C. Jung (New York: Dell,1964), p. 303.

34. Ibid., p. 287.

35. Lecoq, "Le mouvement et le théâtre."

36. Lecoq, Interview, May 1972.

37. Ibid.

38. Ibid.

39. Lecoq, cited in Mounin, *Introduction à la sémiologie*, pp. 176–177.

40. Jacques Lecoq, "Le role de l'improvisation dans l'enseignement de l'art dramatique," *Institut International du Théâtre*, Bucarest, 1964.

41. Lecoq, Interview, May 1972.

42. Lecoq, "L'école Jacques Lecoq," p. 41.

43. Jacques Lecoq, Interview, Paris, July 1971.

44. Lecoq, Stage d'été, July 1971, notes.

45. Lecoq, Interview, May 1972.

46. Lecoq, "Le mouvement et le théâtre."

47. Aljean Harnetz, "Marcel Marceau—Look, Ma, He's Talking," *New York Times*, November 25,1973.

48. Lecoq, Stage d'été, July 1971, notes.

49. Lecoq, Interview, July 1971.

50. Lecoq, "L'école Jacques Lecoq," *Théâtre de la Ville*, p. 42.

51. Lecoq, "L'école Jacques Lecoq," p. 41.

52. Lecoq, Stage d'été, 1971, notes.

53. There is a more complete discussion of Decroux's concept of the neutral mask in chapter 2.

54. Lecoq, Interview, July 1971.

55. Ibid.

56. Lecoq, Stage d'été, 1971, notes.

57. Lecoq, "L'école Jacques Lecoq," *Théâtre de la Ville*, p. 41.

58. Lecoq, Stage d'été, 1971 notes.

59. Lecoq, Stage d'été, 1971, notes.

60. Ibid.

61. Lecoq, "L'école Jacques Lecoq," p. 41.

62. Lecoq, Stage d'été, 1971, notes.

63. Ibid.

64. Lecoq, "Le role de l'improvisation dans l'enseignement de l'art dramatique" p. 139.

65. Lecoq, Stage d'été, 1971, notes.
66. Mounin, *Introduction à la semiologie*, p. 176.
67. Lecoq, Stage d'été, 1971, notes.
68. Jacques Lecoq, L'Ecole Jacques Lecoq brochure.
69. Jacques Lecoq, "Le clown et le dérisoire," Cours Public, presented at Journées internationales du Théâtre des Nations, April 1972.
70. Kolakowski, cited in Jan Kott, *Shakespeare Our Contemporary* (London: Methuen, 1967), p. 141.
71. Lecoq, "Le clown et le dérisoire."
72. Henri Bergson, "Laughter," in *Comedy*, ed. Wylie Sypher (New York: Doubleday Anchor Books, 1956), p. 79.
73. Lecoq, "L'école Jacques Lecoq," p. 42.
74. Lecoq, Stage d'été, 1971, notes.
75. Ibid.
76. Jean Anouilh, cited in Michael Robinson, *The Long Sonata of the Dead* (New York: Grove Press, 1969), p. 248.
77. Ibid., p. 237.
78. Jacques Lecoq, L'Ecole Jacques Lecoq, brochure.

Chapter 7. Conclusion

1. Harold Rosenberg, *The Tradition of the New* (New York: McGraw-Hill, 1965), p. 89.
2. Ibid., pp. 211–12.
3. Ibid., p. 214.
4. Etienne Decroux, *Paroles sur le mime* (Paris: Gallimard: 1963), p. 34.
5. Claude Kipnis, *The Mime Book* (New York: Harper & Row, 1976).

BIBLIOGRAPHY

This bibliography is divided by chapters. There are two subdivisions within each chapter: Books, and Other Sources Consulted. The latter is comprised of articles, interviews, radio programs, lectures, press releases, and program notes. Books are arranged in traditional alphabetical order by author's last name. Other Sources Consulted are arranged chronologically because of the large number of entries in this category for which there was no author or title indicated but only a date of publication.

Chapter 1. Introduction

Books

Aristotle. *On Poetry and Style.* Translated by G. M. A. Grube. New York: Bobbs-Merrill, 1958.

Attinger, Gustav. *L'esprit de la commedia dell'arte dans le théâtre français.* Paris: Librarie théâtrale, 1950.

Broadbent, R. J. *A History of Pantomime.* London: Simkin, Marshall, Hamilton, Kent, 1901.

Christout, Marie Françoise. *Le Merveilleux et le Théâtre du Silence.* Paris: Editions Mouton, 1965.

Copeau, Jacques. *Souvenirs du Vieux Colombier.* Paris: Nouvelles Editions Latines, 1931.

Dick, Kay. *Pierrot.* London: Hutchinson, 1960.

Dorcy, Jean. *A la rencontre de mime et des mimes.* Neuilly sur Seine: Les Cahiers de danse et de culture, 1958.

———. *The Mime.* New York: Robert Speller & Sons, 1961.

———. *J'aime la mime.* Lausanne: Editions del Noël, 1962.

Duchartre, Pierre-Louis. The Italian Comedy. New York: Dover Publications, 1966.

Duerr, Edwin. *The Length and Depth of Acting.* New York: Holt Rinehart & Winston, 1962.

Dullin, Charles. *Souvenirs et notes de travail d'un Acteur.* Paris: Odette Lieutier, 1946.

Findlater, Richard. *Grimaldi: King of Clowns.* London: MacGibbon and Kee, 1955.

Garaudy, Roger. *Danser sa vie.* Paris: Seuil, 1973.

Ginistry, Paul. *Théâtre de la rue.* Paris: Editions Albert Morance, 1925.

Halliday, Andrew. *Comical Fellows.* London: J. H. Thomson, 1863.

Hanlon Lees, Frères. *Memoires et pantomimes des Frères Hanlon Lees.* Paris: Reverchon et Vollet, 1880.

Hébert, George. *L'Education physique par la méthode nautrelle.* 10 vols. Paris: Librarie Vuibert,1949.

Hugounet, Paul. *Mimes et Pierrots.* Paris: Librarie Fischbacher, 1889.

Janin, Jules. *Duburau.* Paris: Librarie des Bibliophiles, 1881.

Jolly, Alison. *The Evolution of Primate B ·havior.* New York: Macmillan, 1972.

Leathers, Victor. *British Entertainers in France.* Toronto: University of Toronto Press, 1959.

Mauss, Marcel. *Manuel d'ethnographie.* Paris: Petite Bibliothèque Payot, 1967.

Mayer, David. *Harlequin in His Element.* Cambridge: Harvard University Press, 1969.

Meyerhold. *Meyerhold on Theatre.* Translated and edited by Edward Braun. New York: Hill & Wang, 1969.

Mic, Constant. *La Commedia dell'arte.* Paris: La Pléiade, 1927.

Nicoll, Allardyce. *Masks, Mimes and Miracles.* New York: Cooper Square Publishers, 1963.

Oreglia, Giacomo. *The Commedia dell'Arte.* New York: Hill & Wang, 1968.

Péricaud, Louis. *Le Théâtre des Funambules.* Paris: Léon Sapin Librarie, 1897.

Plato. *Collected Dialogues.* Edited by Edith Hamilton and Huntington Cairns. New York: Bollingen Foundation, 1961.

Rémy, Tristan. *Jean-Gaspard Deburau.* Paris: L'Arche Editeur, 1954.

Sand, Maurice. *Masques et Buffons.* Paris: Michel Lévy Frères, 1860.

Southern, Richard. *The Seven Ages of the Theatre.* New York: Hill & Wang, 1963.

Other Sources Consulted

Dorcy, Jean. Private interview. Paris: February 1972.

Croce, Arlene. "Dancing." *New Yorker.* 5 August 1974.

Svehla, Jaroslav. "Jean-Gaspard Deburau: The Immortal Pierrot." *Mime Journal,* no. 5 (1977).

Chapter 2. Jacques Copeau

Books

Anders, France. *Jacques Copeau et le Cartel des Quatre.* Paris: A. G. Nizet, 1959.

Bentley, Eric. *In Search of Theatre.* New York: Alfred A. Knopf, 1953.

Borgal, Clément. *Jacques Copeau.* Paris: L'Arche Editeur, 1960.

Copeau, Jacques. *Souvenirs du Vieux Colombier.* Paris: Nouvelle Editions Latines, 1931.

―――. *Le théâtre populaire.* Paris: Presses Universitaires de France, 1942.

―――. *Ecrits sur le théâtre.* Paris: Michel Brient Editeur, 1955.

―――. *Appels.* Paris: Gallimard, 1974.

Doisy, Marcel. *Jacques Copeau.* Paris: Le cercle du livre, 1954.

Hébert, George. *L'Education physique ou l'entrainement complet par la méthode naturelle.* Paris: Librarie Vuibert, 1949.

Kurtz, Maurice. *Jacques Copeau: Biographie d'un théâtre.* Paris: Les Editions Nagel, 1950.

Other Sources Consulted

Copeau, Jacques. "Visites à Gordon Craig, Jacques Dalcroze, et Adolphe Appia." *Revue d'histoire du théâtre,* 15e année (December 1963).

―――. "An Essay on Dramatic Renovation." Translated by Richard Hiatt. *Educational Theatre Journal,* no. 19 (December 1967).

Eldredge, Sears. "Jacques Copeau and the Mask in Actor Training." *Mime, Mask, and Marionette* 2, nos. 3–4 (1979–1980).

Frank, Waldo. "Copeau Begins Again." *Theatre Arts Monthly,* no. 9 (September 1925).

Katz, Albert M. "The Genesis of the Vieux Colombier." *Educational Theatre Journal,* December 1967.

Kusler, Barbara Leigh. "Jacques Copeau's School for Actors." *Mime Journal,* nos. 9 and 10 (1979).

Volbach, Walther. "Jacques Copeau, Appia's Finest Disciple." *Educational Theatre Journal,* no. 3 (October 1965).

Chapter 3. Etienne Decroux

Books

Barrault, Jean-Louis. *Réflexions sur le théâtre.* Paris: J. Vautrain, 1949.

Bentley, Eric. *In Search of Theatre.* New York: Alfred A. Knopf, 1953.

Decroux, Etienne. *Paroles sur le mime.* Paris: Gallimard, 1963.

Dorcy, Jean. *A la rencontre de mime et des mimes.* Neuilly sur Seine: Les Cahiers de danse et de culture, 1958.

Fleming, William. *Art and Ideas.* New York: Holt, Rinehart & Winston, 1963.

Read, Herbert. *A Concise History of Modern Painting.* New York: Frederick A. Praeger, 1965.

Richy, Pierre, and de Mauraige, J. C. *Initiation au mime.* Paris: Editions de l'Amicale, 1968.

Other Sources Consulted

Craig, Edward Gordon. "To Madame Eleonora Duse." *The Mask* 1 (March 1908).

———. "The Actor and the Uber-marionette." *The Mask* 1 (April 1908).

Garcin, Hélène. "Etienne Decroux, Mime de grand talent, formera t-il des mimes et des comédiens?" *Aujourd'hui,* 25 May 1942.

Laurent, Jean. "Etienne Decroux, Un Apôtre du théâtre Muet." *Toute la Vie,* 4 June 1942.

Fournier, Christian. "Par amour de la statuaire humaine, un homme décide d'être muet." *Paris Midi,* 16 July 1942.

Dorcy, Jean. "Jean-Louis Barrault et Etienne Decroux créateurs du mime corporel." *Gavroche* (Nimes), 26 July 1945.

G., R. "La Mime." *18 Juin,* 20 March 1946.

Outie, Claude. "Comédien sans visage, le mime Decroux." *Combat.* 19 June 1946.

Bertrix, Georgette. "Le Mime Decroux." *18 Juin,* 8 August 1946.

"Etienne Decroux, Zélateur du Mime." *Spectateur,* 12 November 1946.

Powell, Dilys. "Films of the Week." *London Times,* 1 December 1946.

Silvant, Jean. "Le Mime Etienne Decroux." *Combat,* 11 December 1946.

Michel, Jacqueline. "Etienne Decroux." *Le Parisien Libéré,* 29 May 1947.

Engelhard, Hubert. "Le Mime Etienne Decroux." *Réforme,* 31 May 1947.

Despremont, Jean. "Trois Mimes français, Etienne Decroux, Jean-Louis Barrault, et Marcel Marceau." *Combat,* 8 November 1947.

Gavroche (Nimes), 14 April 1948.

Hastings, Lily, and Hastings, Baird. "The New Mime of Etienne Decroux." *Dance,* September 1951.

Ravon, Georges. *Figaro Littéraire,* 27 March 1954.

Landry, Robert J. "Paris Dean of Mime at Actors' Studio." *Variety,* 23 October 1957.

Whittaker, Herbert."Man is Master, Theme of Mime by Decroux." *Toronto Globe and Mail,* 3 February 1958.

Epstein, Alvin. "The Mime Theatre of Etienne Decroux." *Chrysalis* 11 nos. 1–2 (1958).

Nicollier, Jean. Des Mimes à une grande ballerine." *Gazette de Lausanne,* 17 April 1959.

Kerr, Walter. "Etienne Decroux Stages 'Mime Theatre' Program." *New York Herald Tribune,* 24 December 1959.

Herridge, Frances. "Decroux Mime Theatre at Cricket." *New York Post,* 24 December 1959.

Gelb, Arthur. "Theatre: Pantomime Art." *New York Times,* 24 December 1959.

Bolton, Whitney. "Master of Mime Offers Good Show." *Morning Telegraph,* 25 December 1959.

Nadel, Norman. "Mime Theatre of Decroux in Carnegie Recital Hall." *New York World Telegram and Sun,* 8 November 1961.

Keane, George. "Three Hours of Dumb Show Not Easy, But Etienne Decroux Never Flinches," *Variety,* 22 November 1961.

Dorcy, Jean. Private interview. Paris, February 1972.

Lust, Annette. "Etienne Decroux: Father of Modern Mime." *Mime Journal* 1 (1974).

Leabhart, Thomas. "An Interview with Decroux." *Mime Journal* 1 (1974).

———. "Etienne Decroux on Masks." *Mime Journal* 2 (1975).

Klier, Vernice. "Etienne Decroux 80th Birthday Interview." *Mime Journal* 7 and 8 (1978).

Dobbels, Daniel. "Entretien: Jean Louis Barrault." *Empreintes* 4 (1980).

———. "Entretien: Yves Marc, Claire Heggen." *Empreintes* 4 (1980).

"Entretien: Yves Lebreton." *Empreintes* 4 (1980).

Tom Leabhart. Private interview. New York, August 1982.

Brown, Tony, and Margolis, Kari. Private interview. New York, October 1982.

Chapter 4. Jean-Louis Barrault

Books

Artaud, Antonin. *The Theatre and Its Double.* Translated by Mary Caroline Richards. New York: Grove Press, 1958.

Barrault, Jean-Louis. *Réflexions sur le théâtre.* Paris: J. Vautrain, 1949.

———. *Nouvelles réflexions sur le théâtre.* Paris: Flammarion, 1959.

————. *The Theatre of Jean-Louis Barrault.* Translated by Joseph Chiari. London: Barrie and Rockliff, 1961.

————. *Souvenirs pour demain.* Paris: Editions du Seuil, 1972.

Bentley, Eric. *In Search of Theatre.* New York: Alfred A. Knopf, 1953.

Bentley, Eric, ed. *The Classic Theatre.* Vol. 3. Garden City: Doubleday Anchor Books, 1959.

Copeau, Jacques. *Appels.* Paris: Gallimard, 1974.

Dorcy, Jean. *A la rencontre de mime et des mimes.* Neuilly sur Seine: Les Cahiers de Danse et de Culture, 1958.

Poesio, Paolo Emilio. *Jean-Louis Barrault.* Bologna: Arti Grafiche Federigo Cappelli.

Other Sources Consulted

Barrault, Jean-Louis. "*Autour d'une mère.*" *La Bête Noire,* June 1935.

Stern. "*Autour d'une mère.*" *Variety,* 19 June 1935.

"*Autour d'une mère.*" Extraits de presse. June 1935.

Brisson, Pierre. "*Numance.*" *Le Figaro,* 25 April 1937.

Altman, Georges. "Drame d'un Peuple—*Numance.*" *Le Peuple,* 4 May 1937.

Priacel, Stefan. "Après 350 ans *Numance.*" *Humanité,* 4 May 1937.

Carr, Philip. "Paris Looks at Spain." *New York Times,* 13 June 1937.

"*La Faim.*" *Le Jour,* 9 April 1939.

Barrault, Jean-Louis, "*La Faim.*" *Le Figaro,* 11 April 1939.

"*La Faim.*" *Paris Soir.* 19 April 1939.

Descaves, Lucien. "*La Faim.*" *Intran,* 20 April 1939.

Antoine. "*Hamlet et la Faim.*" *Journal,* 20 April 1939.

Brisson, Pierre. "Chronique des Spectacles." *Le Figaro,* 23 April 1939.

"L'oeuvre dramatique, *Hamlet et la Faim.*" *L'Oeuvre,* 29 April 1939.

Cremieux, Benjamin. "*Hamlet et la Faim,* au Théâtre de l'Atelier." *La Lumière,* 5 May 1939.

"*Hamlet—La Faim.*" *Gringoire,* 11 May 1939.

Barrault, Jean-Louis, "Art et Technique Dramatiques." *Revue de la quinzaine,* 1 August 1939.

Dorcy, Jean. "Jean-Louis Barrault, Etienne Decroux—Créateurs du mime corporel." *Gavroche* (Nimes), 26 July 1945.

Powell, Dilys. "Films of the Week." *The Times* (London), 1 December 1946.

Lonchampt, Jacques. "J.-L. Barrault Réflexions sur le théâtre." *JMF,* 21 December 1949.

Frank, André. "Jean-Louis Barrault." *Caliban,* no. 40 (June 1950).

Barrault, Jean-Louis. "Entretiens sur le théâtre." *La Revue Théâtrale,* 7ᵉ année, no 19 (1952): 7–21.

———. "Il n'y a que le sang qui compte." *Arts,* 26 June 26 1952.

———. Interview. *Arts,* 12–18 September 1952.

"Notre Companie," "Baptiste," "Les Adieux." Program notes—Companie Renaud-Barrault. Latin American tour, May, June, July 1954.

Dazy René. "Jean-Louis Barrault montera son action dramatique: Tandis que j'agonise." *Libération,* 25–26 September 1954.

Mossu, René. "Jean-Louis Barrault sert de modèle a un pasteur zurichois qui enseigne par mime l'Evangile aux sourds-meuts." *France Soir,* 5 December 1956.

Schiller, W. "Jean-Louis Barrault a donné aux enfants de la reine d'Angleterre une leçon de mime." *France Soir,* 29 November 1956.

Field, Rowland, "Pure Delight." *Newark Evening News,* 19 February 1957.

Bracker, Milton. "A Joyous Au Revoir." *New York Times,* 19 February 1957.

Beaufort, John. *Christian Science Monitor,* 23 February 1957.

Barrault, Jean-Louis. "L'Art du geste." *Cahiers Renaud-Barrault,* no. 20 (October, 1957).

Ghilardi, Fernando. "Omaggio a Jean-Louis Barrault." *Il Dramma,* anno 40, no 330–332 (March–April 1964).

Brooking, Jack. "In the Rehearsal Room with the Barraults." *Players Magazine* 41, no. 1 (October 1964).

Barrault, Jean-Louis. "Scandale et Provocation." *Cahiers Renaud-Barrault,* no. 54 (April 1966).

Pilikan, Holhannes. "Dialogue with Barrault." *Drama* 89 (Summer 1968).

Liebowitz, Bettina. "An Interview with Jean-Louis Barrault." *Cue,* 4 October 1969.

Barrault, Jean-Louis. "Mise en scène de *Autour d'une mère.*" Cahiers Renaud-Barrault, n°71, 1ᵉ trimestre, 1970.

Carlson, Jon. "Reducible to a Single Presence." *Village Voice,* 28 May 1970.

Barrault, Jean-Louis. Interview at Théâtre Recamier by Danièle Marty and William Weiss, Paris, January 1972.

"Madeleine Renaud et Jean-Louis Barrault reçoivent." ORTF radio, Paris, May 1974.

Dobbels, Daniel. "Entretien." *Empreintes,* No. 4 (1980).

Chapter 5. Marcel Marceau

Books

Chaplin, Charles. *My Autobiography.* New York: Simon & Schuster, 1964.

Dorcy, Jean. *A la rencontre de mime et des mimes.* Neuilly sur Seine: Les Cahiers de Danse et de Culture, 1958.

Marceau, Marcel. *The Story of Bip.* New York: Harper & Row, 1976.

Richy, Pierre. *Initiation au mime.* Paris: Editions d l'Amicale, 1960.

———. *Jeux Silencieux.* Paris: Editions de l'Amicale, 1969.

Stanislavski, Constantin. *An Actor Prepares.* Harmondsworth, Middlesex: Penguin Books, 1967.

Other Sources Consulted

"Le Prix Deburau décerné pour la première fois." *Aurore,* 14 July 1945.

Roche. "Marcel Marceau." *Ce Soir,* 12 August 1947.

Lerminier, Georges. "Marcel Marceau et Pierre Sonnier ressuscitent la tradition des funambules." *L'Aube,* 6 June 1949.

"Renouveau de la Pantomine." *La Croix,* 15 April 1950.

"Après J.-L. Barrault, Marceau ressuscite l'art du mime Deburau." *Le Soir,* 16 April 1950.

"La companie Marcel Marceau a installé 'Bip' dans ses meubles." *Action,* 16 April 1950.

Saurel, Renée. "Pantomimes et Mimodrame de Marcel Marceau au studio des Champs Elysées." *Combat,* 18 April 1950.

Alter, André. "Marcel Marceau nous restitue l'art du mime dan toute sa plénitude." *L'Aube,* 19 April 1950.

Triolet, Else. *Les Lettres Françaises,* 20 April 1950.

Reille, Jean-Francis. "Un qui se tait." *Arts,* 21 April 1950.

Vorageolles, Jacques. "Une brève rencontre avec . . . le mime Marceau." *Combat,* 15 June 1950.

"Pendant 3 mois on ne parlera pas sur la scène du studio des Champs Elysées." *Libération,* 5 March 1951.

"Les mimes de Marcel Marceau avec leur masques éclatants." *Combat,* 7 March 1951.

Beigbeder, Marc. "Au studio des Champs Elysées nouvelles pantomimes de Marcel Marceau." *Le Parisien Libéré,* 10 March 1951.

Ransan, André. "Spectacle de Pantomimes." *Ce Matin Le Pays,* 12 March 1951.

"Les Funambules aux Champs-Elysées." *Opéra,* 14 March 1951.

"Un spectacle de Pantomimes." *France Soir,* 14 March 1951.

Reille, Jean-Francis. "Companie Marcel Marceau." *Arts,* 16 March 1951.

"Un spectacle de Pantomimes." *La Croix,* 17 March 1951.

Cézan, Claude. "Le Mime Marceau." *Les Nouvelles Littéraires,* 22 March 1951.

New York Herald Tribune, 27 April 1951.

"Art de Marcel Marceau." Program—Théâtre Sarah-Bernhardt. 1952 Season.

"Le Théâtre Sarah-Bernhardt va faire renaître les grands spectacles de mimes." *France Soir,* 17 June 1952.

"Le mime Marcel Marceau et sa companie vont presenter un nouveau spectacle à Sarah Bernhardt." *Ce Soir,* 17 June 1952.

"Marceau: Pierrot de Montmartre." *Arts,* 19 June 1952.

Marceau, Marcel. "Je renoue à Sarah-Bernhardt avec la tradition de Deburau." *Combat,* 20 June 1952.

Libération, 24 June 1952.

M., H. "Deux mots avant plusieurs gestes du mime Marceau." *Le Monde,* 25 June 1952.

"Au Theatre Sarah-Bernhardt Marcel Marceau ou la renaissance de l'art muet." *L'Aurore,* 26 June 1952.

Beigbeder, Marc. "Marcel Marceau affirme la royauté du mime." *Le Parisien Libéré,* 26 June 1952.

Triolet, Elsa. "Spectacle Marcel Marceau." *Lettres Françaises,* 4 July 1952.

Lemarchand, Jacques. *Le Figaro,* 5 July 1952.

Dornand, Guy. "Marceau: Un grand mime du Boulevard." *Libération,* 23 September 1952.

"Art de Marcel Marceau." Program—Théâtre de Champs Elysées, 1953.

"Charles Chaplin cable à Marcel Marceau: 'Je viendrai à Paris applaudir vos pantomimes.'" *Paris-Presse,* 29 May 1953.

Salacrou, Armand. "Allez-y Marceau! Nous vous regardons." *Arts,* 29 May 1953.

Lerminier, Georges. "Marcel Marceau et sa companie de mimes ressuscitent les funambules." *Le Parisien,* 30–31 May 1953.

Dornand, Guy. "Marcel Marceau et ses Pantomimes." *Libération,* 1 June 1953.

Rémy, Tristan. "La Pantomime Muette, et le mime Marcel Marceau." *L'Humanité Dimanche,* 17 June 1953.

Farrell, Isolde. "Paris Priest of Pantomime." *New York Times,* 20 September 1953.

Program—Théâtre de la Renaissance, Paris, 1954.

Marceau, Marcel. "L'Art du mime et de la Pantomime." Program—Théâtre de la Comédie. Geneva, 1954.

"Le retour de Marcel Marceau." *Lettres Françaises,* 27 May 1954.

Dornand, Guy. "Bip—frère de Charlot ou Marcel Marceau au théâtre de la renaissance." *Libération,* 5–6 June 1954.

B., C. "Au théâtre de la renaissance—Marcel Marceau." *Le Figaro,* 5 June 1954.

Beigbeder, Marc. "Bip repetita placent. . . ." *Lettres Françaises,* 10 June 1954.

de Garambé, B. "Le mime Marcel Marceau enchaine 'la lune et la terre.'" *Le Théâtre,* 10 June 1954.

Demeron, Pierre. "Les Pantomimes, Burlesques Pathétiques." *Aspects de la France,* 11 June 1954.

Chabrol, Jean-Pierre. "Lettre à l'homme qui s'est arraché la langue." *L'Humanité Dimanche,* 27 June 1954.

Dubreuilh, Simone. "Marcel Marceau héritier de Charlie Chaplin." *Libération,* 15 July 1954.

Simon, Louis. "Pour ou Contre le pantomime." *Témoignage Chrétien,* 23 July 1954.

"Présentation d'un mime au monde entier." *Combat* 23 October 1954.

"Lettres Françaises, 25 December 1954.

Paviot, Paul. "Un Film sur l'art du silence." *Lettres Françaises,* 29 December 1954.

Marceau, Marcel. "Théâtre du Nouveau Monde." Program. Canada, 1955.

Publicity Release. Jean de Rigault. Montreal, 1955.

Publicity Release. Ronald Wilford Associates, 1955. "The Marcel Marceau Story," "The Language of the Heart," "The Art of Marcel Marceau," "The Art of Mime."

Program—Phoenix Theater, New York, 1955.

Atkinson, Brooks. "The Theater: M. Marceau." *New York Times,* 22 September 1955.

———. "The Theater: M. Marceau." *New York Times,* 2 February 1956.

Bergeron, Régis. "Marcel Marceau." 5 April 1956.

Program—Théâtre de l'Ambigu. Paris, 1956.

Rélations avec la Presse, Théâtre de l'Ambigu, 1956.

Marceau, Marcel. "Voici mes publics." *Arts,* 11 April 1956.

"Le mime Marceau." *Parisien,* 28 April 1956.

C., G. F. "Marceau, nouveau Deburau sur le boulevard du crime." *Le Monde,* 28 April 1956.

"Marcel Marceau, Ancien décorateur sur porcelaine a ressuscité la pantomime." *Presse,* 1 May 1956.

Gautier, Jean-Jacques. "A L'Ambigu, Le mime Marcel Marceau et sa companie." *Le Figaro,* 4 May 1956.

Megret, Christian. "Marceau l'admirable." *Carrefour,* 9 May 1956.

Kemp, Robert. "Marcel Marceau à l'Ambigu." *Le Monde,* 11 May 1956.

Ch., R. "Marcel Marceau au Théâtre de l'Ambigu." *Paris* Presse, 11 May 1956.

Dornand, Guy. "Marcel Marceau ou: le triomphe du silence." *La Libération,* 14 May 1956.

Nouvelles Littératures, 17 May 1956.

Kantors, Robert. "Cela va sans dire." *Express,* 18 May 1956.

Marcabru, Pierre. "Le mime Marceau." *Arts,* 23–29 May 1956.

Paglio, François. *Temps Chrétien,* 8 June 1956.

Guth, Paul. *Le Figaro Littéraire,* 23 June 1956.

Bloch, Gilbert. "La rentrée de Marcel Marceau à l'Ambigu." *Humanité,* 13 September 1956.

Jhering, Herbert. "Die Weltkunst der Pantomime." *Ein Gesprach,* 4⁰, August 1956.

Cartier, Jacqueline. "Marceau: Un art qui a les pied sur le sol." 1958.

Marcabru, Pierre. "Le mime reconquiert le Boulevard." *Arts,* 24 September 1958.

A., J. "Trois images: des mois de travail." *Paris Journal,* 2 October 1958.

Bloch, Gilbert. *Humanité,* 6 October 1958.

Marcabru, Pierre. "Marcel Marceau: L'Esprit avant le coeur." *Arts,* 8 October 1958.

Vallaire, Stephen. "Marcel Marceau, Moissonneur de l'espace." *Lettres Françaises,* 9 October 1958.

Megret, Christian. "Etonnant Marceau." *Carrefour,* 9 October 1958.

Delorh, Bertrand. "L'Ambigu, Marcel Marceau." *Réforme,* 11 October 1958.

Gilles, Edmond. "Dialogue avec Marceau sur l'art du geste et du silence." *Humanité,* 6 February 1959.

Brillant, Marie. "Sire le geste." *La Croix,* 8 February 1959.

"Marcel Marceau pratique l'art de tout dire sans prononcer un mot." *La Presse Magazine,* 19 May 1959.

Program—San Juan Drama Festival, February 1961.

Davis, R. G. "Method in Mime." *Tulane Drama Review* 6, no. 4 (Summer 1962).

Bolton, Whitney. "Marceau Returns as Brilliant as Ever." *Morning Telegraph,* 3 January 1963.

Bart, Peter. "A Quiet Pinocchio Prepared for T.V." *New York Times,* 11 December 1964.

Gent, George. "Mime Meets Clown." *New York Times,* 31 January 1965.

Marcel Marceau Press Book, 1965–66, U.S.A.

Rudiger, Reinhold. "Im Gesprach mit Marcel Marceau." *Teater Heute,* no. 7 (July 1965).

Program—Edinburgh International Festival, 1967.

"The Origins of Bip." Saville Theatre Program, 1967.

Cox, Rebecca. "Marcel Marceau Speaks." *Prompt,* no. 11 (1968), pp. 9–11.

Bunce, Alan. "The French Emissary of Mime." *The Christian Science Monitor,* 8 May 1970.

The Mime of Marcel Marceau. Learning Corporation of America, 1972.

Program—Théâtre de la Ville. Paris, March 21–April 15, 1972.

Marceau, Marcel. Lecture-demonstration. Théâtre des Nations. Paris, April 1972.

Barnes, Clive. "Stage: Refined Marceau." *New York Times,* 20 April 1973.

Corry, John. "Marceau Explains Aim of his Miming." *New York Times,* 4 May 1973.

Program—City Center New York. April–May, 1973.

Marceau, Marcel. Lecture-demonstration. Brooklyn College, May 1973.

Harnetz, Aljean. "Marcel Marceau—Look, Ma, He's Talking." *New York Times,* 25 November 1973.

Weiler, A. H. "Marceau in Dual Role in *Shanks.*" *New York Times,* 10 October 1974.

Shanks. Production information. Paramount Pictures Corporation, 1974.

Dembart, Lee. "Marceau Adds Words to the Music of Motion." *New York Times,* 18 October 1974.

Gottfried, Martin. "Marceau Quietly Returns." *New York Post,* 26 March 1975.

Barnes, Clive. "Inimitable Marceau! Vive La Meme Chose." *New York Times,* 26 March 1975.

———. "Marceau's Lyric Poems of Movement." *New York Times,* 6 April 1975.

Chapter 6. Jacques Lecoq

Books

Aristotle. *On Poetry and Style.* Translated by G. M. A. Grube. New York: Bobbs-Merrill, 1958.

Beals, Ralph L., and Hoijer, Harry. *An Introduction to Anthropology.* New York: Macmillan, 1964.

Bergson, Henri. *Comedy*. Garden City, N.Y.: Doubleday Anchor Books, 1956.

Dorcy, Jean. *A la recontre de mime et des mimes*. Neuilly sur Seine: Les Cahiers de Danse et de Culture, 1958.

Jolly, Alison. *The Evolution of Primate Behavior*. New York; Macmillan, 1972.

Jousse, Marcel. *L'Anthropologie du geste*. Paris: Resma, 1960.

Jung, Carl C., ed. *Man and his Symbols*. New York: Dell 1968.

Kott, Jan. *Shakespeare Our Contemporary*. London: Methuen, 1967.

Mounin, Georges. *Introduction à la Sémiologie*. Paris: Les Editions de minuit, 1970.

Robinson, Michael. *The Long Sonata of the Dead*. New York: Grove Press, 1969.

Other Sources Consulted

"Voyage autour du mime." Program teatro Quirino. Rome, March 1959.

Lecoq, Jacques. "Le role de l'improvisation dans l'ensignement de l'art dramatique." Lecture-demonstration for l'Institut Internationale du Théâtre. Bucarest, 1964.

———. "Le Mouvement et le Théâtre." *ATAC Informations*, no. 13 (December 1967).

———. "Rittorno a l'espressione fisica dell'attore." Program of the Biennale de Venezia, 17–19 September 1969.

———. "Le corps et son image." *Architecture d'Aujourd'hui*, no. 152 (October-November 1970).

Syllabus for Stage d'été. Paris, 1971.

Personal notes. Stage d'été. Paris, 1971.

Lecoq, Jacques. Private interview. Paris, July 1971.

Brochure Ecole Lecoq, 1972–1973.

Lecoq, Jacques. "Ecole Jacques Lecoq au Théâtre de la Ville." *Journal du Théâtre de la Ville*, January 1972.

Gautier, Philippe. "Stage Enseignement Théâtre." *Journal du Théâtre de la Ville*, March 1972.

Rolfe, Bari. "The Mime of Jacques Lecoq." *The Drama Review* 16, no. 1 (March 1972).

Lecoq, Jacques. "Présentation des clowns au Théâtre des Nations." Paris, 26 April 1972.

———. Private interview. Paris, May 1972.

Robertson, Nan. "Body Language Helps U.S. Professor Read French Psyche and his Own." *New York Times*, 26 June 1973.

Rolfe, Bari. "Masks, Mimes and Mummenschanz." *Mime Journal*, no. 2 (1975).

Chapter 7. Conclusion

Books

Kipnis, Claude. *The Mime Book.* New York: Harper & Row, 1974.
Rosenberg, Harold. *The Tradition of the New.* New York: McGraw-Hill, 1965.

INDEX